经济管理类专业
大数据技术与应用实验教程

Experiment Course of Big Data Technology and Application for
University Students Majoring in Economics and Management

郭明晶　肖扬　欧阳剑　编著

图书在版编目(CIP)数据

经济管理类专业大数据技术与应用实验教程/郭明晶等编著. —武汉:中国地质大学出版社,2021.9
ISBN 978-7-5625-5119-5

Ⅰ.①经⋯
Ⅱ.①郭⋯
Ⅲ.①数据处理-应用-经济管理-高等学校-教材
Ⅳ.①F2-39

中国版本图书馆 CIP 数据核字(2021)第 194231 号

经济管理类专业大数据技术与应用实验教程		郭明晶　肖扬　欧阳剑		**编著**
责任编辑:马　严	选题策划:毕克成　张晓红　王凤林			责任校对:何澍语

出版发行:中国地质大学出版社(武汉市洪山区鲁磨路388号)　　　　　　邮编:430074
电　　话:(027)67883511　　　传　　真:(027)67883580　　　E-mail:cbb@cug.edu.cn
经　　销:全国新华书店　　　　　　　　　　　　　　　　　　　　　　http://cugp.cug.edu.cn

开本:787 毫米×1092 毫米　1/16　　　　　　　　　字数:225 千字　　印张:9.75
版次:2021 年 9 月第 1 版　　　　　　　　　　　　　印次:2021 年 9 月第 1 次印刷
印刷:湖北睿智印务有限公司
ISBN 978-7-5625-5119-5　　　　　　　　　　　　　　　　　　　　　　定价:38.00 元

如有印装质量问题请与印刷厂联系调换

目　录

第一章　大数据分布式技术原理 …………………………………………………（1）
　　实验 1　大数据平台搭建——搭建 3 节点 hadoop 分布式集群实验 …………（1）
第二章　大数据分布式计算框架 …………………………………………………（15）
　　实验 2　大数据平台搭建——MapReduce 进行文本词频统计实验 …………（15）
第三章　大数据采集 ………………………………………………………………（24）
　　实验 3　大数据信息采集——使用 Flume 完成用户收视数据的收集 ………（24）
　　实验 4　爬虫实验-大数据信息采集——使用 Request 进行二手房网站信息
　　　　　　爬取和初步分析 …………………………………………………………（41）
第四章　大数据管理 ………………………………………………………………（50）
　　实验 5　大数据的预处理——收视数据的小文件合并实验 …………………（50）
　　实验 6　大数据的预处理——编写 MR 程序对原始的收视数据进行清洗与预
　　　　　　处理实验 …………………………………………………………………（59）
第五章　商业大数据分析 …………………………………………………………（78）
　　实验 7　大数据分析——利用 hive 对预处理后的收视数据进行统计分析实验
　　　　　　………………………………………………………………………………（78）
　　实验 8　sqoop 安装部署及数据结果利用 hdfs 导入实验 ……………………（84）
　　实验 9　sqoop 安装部署及数据结果利用 hdfs 导出实验 ……………………（99）
第六章　商业大数据挖掘方法 ……………………………………………………（116）
　　实验 10　大数据挖掘——电子商务数据的逻辑回归模型挖掘实验 ………（116）
　　实验 11　大数据挖掘——电子商务数据的决策树分类模型挖掘实验 ……（119）
　　实验 12　大数据挖掘——利用 Apriori 算法进行电子商务数据的关联规则挖
　　　　　　 掘实验 ……………………………………………………………………（125）
　　实验 13　大数据挖掘——利用 K-means 算法进行数据挖掘实验 …………（131）
　　实验 14　大数据挖掘实战案例——利用大数据挖掘实现电影广告的精准营销
　　　　　　 ……………………………………………………………………………（137）
第七章　大数据可视化 ……………………………………………………………（141）
　　实验 15　大数据可视化——使用 Matplotlib 进行可视化操作练习 ………（141）
　　实验 16　大数据可视化实战案例——利用 Matplotlib 分析自行车租赁情况
　　　　　　 ……………………………………………………………………………（147）

第一章　大数据分布式技术原理

实验1　大数据平台搭建
——搭建3节点 hadoop 分布式集群实验

一、实验介绍

本次课程我们使用 hadoop V2.6.0 版本配置3节点的 hadoop 集群。

二、实验原理

YARN 基础架构概述。

1. Resource Manager(RM)

Resource Manager(RM)接收客户端任务请求,接收和监控 Node Manager(NM)的资源情况汇报,负责资源的分配与调度,启动和监控 Application Master(AM)。

2. Node Manager

Node Manager 节点上的资源管理,启动 container 运行 task 计算,资源、container 情况汇报给 RM,任务处理情况汇报给 AM。

3. Application Master

Application Master 单个 Application(Job)的 task 管理和调度,向 RM 进行资源的申请,向 NM 发出 launch container 指令,接收 NM 的 task 处理状态信息。

4. Web Application Proxy

Web Application Proxy 用于防止 YARN 遭受 Web 攻击,本身是 Resource Manager 的一部分,可通过配置独立进程。Resource Manager Web 的访问基于受信用户,当 Application Master 运行于一个非受信用户,其提供给 Resource Manager 的可能是非受信连接,Web Application Proxy 可以阻止这种连接提供给 RM。

5. Job History Server

Node Manager 在启动的时候会初始化 Log Aggregation Service 服务，该服务会在把本机执行的 container log（在 container 结束的时候）收集并存放到 hdfs 指定的目录下。Application Master 会把 job history 信息写到 hdfs 的 job history 临时目录下，并在结束的时候把 job hisoty 移动到最终目录，这样就同时支持了 job 的 recovery. History 会启动 web 和 RPC 服务，用户可以通过网页或 RPC 方式获取作业的信息。

三、实验要求

本次实验会分配 3 个地址，类似 namenode(10.42.78.231)、datanode1(10.42.177.17)、datanode2(10.42.92.29)。

每个人分配到的 IP 可能不同。在实验过程中，涉及写 IP 地址的部分，大家要根据自己分配到的 IP 地址，修改 namenode、datanode1 和 datanode2 的相应地址。

查看自己分配到的 IP 地址如下图所示：

首先我们要对主机、软件、用户、目录做一个规划。

1）主机规划

	namenode	datanote1	datanote2
namenode	是	否	否
datanode	是	是	是
Resource Manager	是	否	否

2）软件规划

软件	版本	位数
jdk	jdk1.7	64 位
hadoop	Apache hadoop2.6	

3）用户规划

namenode、datanode1 以及 datanode2 的用户和用户组均为 hadoop。

4）目录规划

所有数据和日志目录 /hadoop/data/。

注意：本实验需要按照"hadoop:单机安装配置"部署后继续进行操作,因此必须先完成"hadoop:单机安装配置"实验;所有操作都在hadoop用户下进行操作。

四、实验步骤

(一)实验前准备

1. 首先切入到 hadoop 用户并进行如下操作(所有节点)

```
$ su - hadoop
口令输入:hadoop

$ bash
$ echo $HADOOP_HOME
/hadoop/hadoop
上述输出确认hadoop的环境变量设置有效,如果无效则激活环境变量:
$ source ~/.bash_profile
```

2. 新建 hadoop 数据和日志目录(所有节点)

```
$ mkdir /hadoop/data
```

3. 修改 hosts 文件(所有节点)

```
修改配置文件,口令输入:hadoop
hadoop@3778f8dee940:~ $ sudo vi /etc/hosts
[sudo] password for hadoop:
```

将下列内容添加至 hosts 文件中的头部:
添加时注意下面两点:
(1)注意将节点对应 IP 更改为自己分配到的 IP 地址。
(2)添加内容插入到 hosts 文件的顶部位置。

```
## hadoop nodes###
10.42.78.231 namenode
```

```
10.42.177.17 datanode1
10.42.92.29 datanode2
# # end hadoop# # #
```

添加完的 hosts 文件内容类似下面的样式:

```
# # hadoop nodes# # #
10.42.78.231 namenode
10.42.177.17 datanode1
10.42.92.29 datanode2
# # end hadoop# # #

127.0.0.1       localhost
::1     localhost ip6-localhost ip6-loopback
fe00::0 ip6-localnet
ff00::0 ip6-mcastprefix
ff02::1 ip6-allnodes
ff02::2 ip6-allrouters

10.42.202.173   58f771c2f442
```

4. 配置 ssh 免密码通信

(1)首先启动 ssh(所有节点)。

```
hadoop@ 357987c120a9:~ $ sudo service ssh start
[ ok ] Starting OpenBSD Secure Shell server: sshd.
hadoop@ 357987c120a9:~ $
```

(2)该环境的 ssh 免密码登录已经配置好,请输入如下命令进行验证(namenode 节点)。

在 namenode 节点上执行下面的命令:
(验证登录是否还需要密码,第一次需要输入 yes,以后不需要密码就可以登录)

```
hadoop@ eb108126bc74:~ $ ssh namenode
hadoop@ eb108126bc74:~ $ exit
```

```
hadoop@ eb108126bc74:~ $ ssh datanode1
hadoop@ eb108126bc74:~ $ exit


hadoop@ eb108126bc74:~ $ ssh datanode2
hadoop@ eb108126bc74:~ $ exit
```

```
hadoop@d8dbf809c9e0:~$ ssh datanode1
The authenticity of host 'datanode1 (10.42.177.17)' can't be established.
ECDSA key fingerprint is 33:5d:12:e4:d5:59:8b:a3:a3:46:45:fd:16:f7:51:c8.
Are you sure you want to continue connecting (yes/no)? yes
Warning: Permanently added 'datanode1,10.42.177.17' (ECDSA) to the list of known hosts.

The programs included with the Debian GNU/Linux system are free software;
the exact distribution terms for each program are described in the
individual files in /usr/share/doc/*/copyright.

Debian GNU/Linux comes with ABSOLUTELY NO WARRANTY, to the extent
permitted by applicable law.
Last login: Wed May  9 22:39:01 2018 from localhost
$
```

```
Connection to datanode1 closed.
hadoop@d8dbf809c9e0:~$ ssh datanode2
The authenticity of host 'datanode2 (10.42.92.29)' can't be established.
ECDSA key fingerprint is 33:5d:12:e4:d5:59:8b:a3:a3:46:45:fd:16:f7:51:c8.
Are you sure you want to continue connecting (yes/no)? yes
Warning: Permanently added 'datanode2,10.42.92.29' (ECDSA) to the list of known hosts.

The programs included with the Debian GNU/Linux system are free software;
the exact distribution terms for each program are described in the
individual files in /usr/share/doc/*/copyright.

Debian GNU/Linux comes with ABSOLUTELY NO WARRANTY, to the extent
permitted by applicable law.
Last login: Wed May  9 22:39:01 2018 from localhost
$
```

注意：出现如上打印信息则证明 ssh 免密码登录成功，成功跳过步骤(3)，否则进行步骤(3)。

(3) 配置 3 节点免密码登录。

① namenode 节点

```
hadoop@ 3778f8dee940:~ $ ssh-keygen -t rsa    # 一路回车
hadoop@ 3778f8dee940:~ $ cat .ssh/id_rsa.pub >> .ssh/authorized_keys
hadoop@ 3778f8dee940:~ $ chmod 600 .ssh/authorized_keys
```

将 authorized_keys 文件复制到 datanode1 和 datanode2 节点，命令如下：

```
hadoop@ 3778f8dee940:~ $ scp ~/.ssh/authorized_keys hadoop@ datanode1:~/
hadoop@ 3778f8dee940:~ $ scp ~/.ssh/authorized_keys hadoop@ datanode2:~/
```

如果提示输入 yes/no 的时候，输入 yes，回车
密码是：hadoop

② datanode1 和 datanode2 节点

```
hadoop@ 3778f8dee940:~ $ ssh-keygen -t rsa    # 一路回车
```

```
hadoop@ 3778f8dee940:~ $ mv authorized_keys ~/.ssh/
hadoop@ 3778f8dee940:~ $ chmod 600 .ssh/authorized_keys
```

③验证免密码登录(namenode 节点)

在 namenode 节点上执行下面的命令：

(验证登录是否还需要密码，第一次需要输入 yes，以后不需要密码就可以登录)

```
hadoop@ eb108126bc74:~ $ ssh datanode1
hadoop@ eb108126bc74:~ $ ssh datanode2
```

```
hadoop@d8bf809c9e0:~$ ssh datanode1
The authenticity of host 'datanode1 (10.42.177.17)' can't be established.
ECDSA key fingerprint is 33:5d:12:e4:d5:59:8b:a3:a3:46:45:fd:16:f7:51:c8.
Are you sure you want to continue connecting (yes/no)? yes
Warning: Permanently added 'datanode1,10.42.177.17' (ECDSA) to the list of known hosts.

The programs included with the Debian GNU/Linux system are free software;
the exact distribution terms for each program are described in the
individual files in /usr/share/doc/*/copyright.

Debian GNU/Linux comes with ABSOLUTELY NO WARRANTY, to the extent
permitted by applicable law.
Last login: Wed May  9 22:39:01 2018 from localhost
$
```

```
Connection to datanode1 closed.
hadoop@d8bf809c9e0:~$ ssh datanode2
The authenticity of host 'datanode2 (10.42.92.29)' can't be established.
ECDSA key fingerprint is 33:5d:12:e4:d5:59:8b:a3:a3:46:45:fd:16:f7:51:c8.
Are you sure you want to continue connecting (yes/no)? yes
Warning: Permanently added 'datanode2,10.42.92.29' (ECDSA) to the list of known hosts.

The programs included with the Debian GNU/Linux system are free software;
the exact distribution terms for each program are described in the
individual files in /usr/share/doc/*/copyright.

Debian GNU/Linux comes with ABSOLUTELY NO WARRANTY, to the extent
permitted by applicable law.
Last login: Wed May  9 22:39:01 2018 from localhost
$
```

(二)搭建 hadoop 集群

在 hadoop 用户登录的环境中进行下列操作。

1. 修改配置文件(namenode 节点)

1)在 namenode 节点上配置 hdfs

(1)修改 core-site.xml。

```
$ cd /hadoop/hadoop/etc/hadoop
$ vi core-site.xml
```

将下面的配置放入＜configuration＞＜/configuration＞标签中间。

```
<property>
  <name>fs.defaultFS</name>
  <value>hdfs://namenode:9000</value>
</property>
<property>
  <name>hadoop.tmp.dir</name>
  <value>/hadoop/tmp</value>
</property>
```

说明：

fs.defaultFS：这里的值指的是默认的 hdfs 路径，取名为 namenode，da 端口号为 9000。

hadoop.tmp.dir：hadoop 的临时目录，如果需要配置多个目录，需要逗号隔开，data 目录需要自己创建。

(2)在 namenode 节点上配置 hdfs-site.xml。

```
$ vi hdfs-site.xml
  <property>
      <name>dfs.replication</name>
      <value>3</value>
  </property>
  <property>
      <name>dfs.permissions</name>
      <value>false</value>
  </property>
  <property>
      <name>dfs.permissions.enabled</name>
      <value>false</value>
  </property>
```

(3)在 namenode 节点上配置 hadoop-env.sh。

```
$ vi hadoop-env.sh
# The java implementation to use.
# export JAVA_HOME=${JAVA_HOME}

export JAVA_HOME=/usr/lib/jvm/java-7-openjdk-amd64
```

```
# The only required environment variable is JAVA_HOME.  All others are
# optional.  When running a distributed configuration it is best to
# set JAVA_HOME in this file, so that it is correctly defined on
# remote nodes.

# The java implementation to use.
export JAVA_HOME=/usr/lib/jvm/java-7-openjdk-amd64
```

2）在 namenode 节点上配置 slaves

```
$ vi slaves
将 slaves 下的 localhos 删除,并加入如下信息：
namenode
datanode1
datanode2
```

3）在 namenode 节点上向其他两个节点分发 hadoop 安装包

```
当出现是否确认连接时输入 yes 即可
Are you sure you want to continue connecting (yes/no)?

$ scp -r /hadoop/hadoop hadoop@ datanode1:/hadoop
$   scp -r /hadoop/hadoop hadoop@ datanode2:/hadoop
```

2. hdfs 配置完毕后启动

1）首先在主节点上进行格式化（namenode）

```
首先进入 hadoop 目录
$  cd /hadoop/hadoop

进行格式化
$  bin/hdfs namenode -format
```

2）在主节点上一键启动 hdfs 所有相关进程（namenode 节点）

```
$  cd /hadoop/hadoop
$  sbin/start-dfs.sh
当出现是否确认连接时输入 yes 即可
Are you sure you want to continue connecting (yes/no)? yes
```

第一章 大数据分布式技术原理

```
hadoop@d8dbf809c9e0:~/hadoop$ sbin/start-dfs.sh
18/06/01 05:32:18 WARN util.NativeCodeLoader: Unable to load native-hadoop library for your platform... using builtin-java classes where applicable
Starting namenodes on [namenode]
The authenticity of host 'namenode (10.42.78.231)' can't be established.
ECDSA key fingerprint is 33:5d:12:e4:d5:59:8b:a3:a3:46:45:fd:16:f7:51:c8.
Are you sure you want to continue connecting (yes/no)? yes
namenode: Warning: Permanently added 'namenode,10.42.78.231' (ECDSA) to the list of known hosts.
namenode: starting namenode, logging to /hadoop/hadoop/logs/hadoop-hadoop-namenode-d8dbf809c9e0.out
namenode: starting datanode, logging to /hadoop/hadoop/logs/hadoop-hadoop-datanode-d8dbf809c9e0.out
datanode1: starting datanode, logging to /hadoop/hadoop/logs/hadoop-hadoop-datanode-ce8fbec3cca8.out
datanode2: starting datanode, logging to /hadoop/hadoop/logs/hadoop-hadoop-datanode-5c265b9d3b1d.out
Starting secondary namenodes [0.0.0.0]
0.0.0.0: starting secondarynamenode, logging to /hadoop/hadoop/logs/hadoop-hadoop-secondarynamenode-d8dbf809c9e0.out
18/06/01 05:32:36 WARN util.NativeCodeLoader: Unable to load native-hadoop library for your platform... using builtin-java classes where applicable
hadoop@d8dbf809c9e0:~/hadoop$
```

3）验证是否启动成功（所有节点）

使用 jps 命令查看，下图分别为 namenode、datanode1、datanode2 的进程启动情况：

  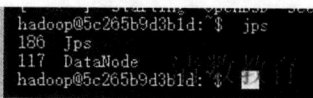

4）上传文件至 hdfs(namenode 节点)

首先我们创建一个目录：

$ mkdir /hadoop/hadoop-data/

$ cd /hadoop/hadoop-data/

我们先创建一个 test.txt 文件，写入如下内容：

$ vi test.txt

hadoop hive hadoop

MapReduce

hdfs hdfs hadoop

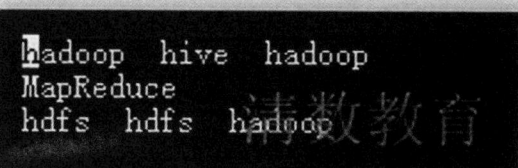

上传至 hdfs：

$ hadoop fs -put test.txt /

$ hadoop fs -ls /

$ hadoop fs -cat /test.txt

· 9 ·

```
hadoop@d8dbf809c9e0:~/hadoop-data$ hadoop fs -put test.txt /
18/06/01 05:35:41 WARN util.NativeCodeLoader: Unable to load native-hadoop library for your pl
ing builtin-java classes where applicable
hadoop@d8dbf809c9e0:~/hadoop-data$ hadoop fs -ls /
18/06/01 05:35:50 WARN util.NativeCodeLoader: Unable to load native-hadoop library for your pl
ing builtin-java classes where applicable
Found 1 items
-rw-r--r--   3 hadoop supergroup         48 2018-06-01 05:35 /test.txt
hadoop@d8dbf809c9e0:~/hadoop-data$ hadoop fs -cat /test.txt
18/06/01 05:35:56 WARN util.NativeCodeLoader: Unable to load native-hadoop library for your pl
ing builtin-java classes where applicable
hadoop hive hadoop

MapReduce

hdfs hdfs hadoop
hadoop@d8dbf809c9e0:~/hadoop-data$
```

3. YARN 安装配置(namenode 节点)

1)在 namenode 节点上配置 mapred-site.xml

```
$ cd /hadoop/hadoop/etc/hadoop
$ cp mapred-site.xml.template mapred-site.xml
$ vi mapred-site.xml

    < property>
        < name> mapreduce.framework.name< /name>
        < value> yarn< /value>
    < /property>
```

2)在 namenode 节点上配置 yarn-site.xml

```
$ viyarn-site.xml

    < property>
        < name> yarn.resourcemanager.connect.retry-interval.ms< /name>
        < value> 2000< /value>
    < /property>
    < property>
        < name> yarn.resourcemanager.hostname< /name>
        < value> namenode< /value>
    < /property>
    < property>
        < name> yarn.resourcemanager.address< /name>
        < value> namenode:8032< /value>
    < /property>
    < property>
```

```
        < name> yarn.resourcemanager.scheduler.address< /name>
        < value> namenode:8034< /value>
    < /property>
    < property>
        < name> yarn.resourcemanager.webapp.address< /name>
        < value> namenode:8088< /value>
    < /property>
    < property>
        < name> yarn.nodemanager.aux-services< /name>
        < value> mapreduce_shuffle< /value>
    < /property>
    < property>
        < name> yarn.nodemanager.aux-services.mapreduce_shuffle.class< /name>
        < value> org.apache.hadoop.mapred.ShuffleHandler< /value>
    < /property>
     < property>
        < name> yarn.nodemanager.resource.memory-mb< /name>
       < value> 2048< /value>
    < /property>
    < property>
    < name> yarn.scheduler.minimum-allocation-mb< /name>
        < value> 512< /value>
    < /property>
    < property>
        < name> yarn.nodemanager.vmem-pmem-ratio< /name>
        < value> 2.1< /value>
< /property>
```

4. 在 namenode 节点上将修改的配置文件分发至其他节点

```
$ scp mapred-site.xmlhadoop@ datanode1:~ /hadoop/etc/hadoop
$ scp mapred-site.xml hadoop@ datanode2:~ /hadoop/etc/hadoop

$ scpyarn-site.xml hadoop@ datanode1:~ /hadoop/etc/hadoop
$ scpyarn-site.xml hadoop@ datanode2:~ /hadoop/etc/hadoop
```

5. 在 namenode 节点上启动 YARN

1）在 namenode 节点上执行

```
$ cd /hadoop/hadoop
$ sbin/start-yarn.sh
```

2）验证启动成功（所有节点）

用 jps 查看进程，发现 namenode 的 Resource Manager 已经启动，以及每个节点的 Node Manager 均启动成功。

使用 jps 命令查看，如下图分别为 namenode、datanode、datanode2 的进程启动情况：

五、实验结果

1. 查看到集群的节点情况，以证明集群的有效性（任何节点均可）

```
# 执行 hadoop 管理命令，输出结果中可以看到一个活动节点的信息
$ hadoop dfsadmin -report
```

```
Name: 10.42.78.231:50010   (d8dbf809c9e0)
Hostname: d8dbf809c9e0
Decommission Status : Normal
Configured Capacity: 84415266816 (78.62 GB)
DFS Used: 45056 (44 KB)
Non DFS Used: 27943763968 (26.02 GB)
DFS Remaining: 56471457792 (52.59 GB)
DFS Used%: 0.00%
DFS Remaining%: 66.90%
Configured Cache Capacity: 0 (0 B)
Cache Used: 0 (0 B)
Cache Remaining: 0 (0 B)
Cache Used%: 100.00%
Cache Remaining%: 0.00%
Xceivers: 1
Last contact: Fri Jun 01 05:44:37 UTC 2018

Name: 10.42.177.17:50010   (datanode1)
Hostname: ce8fbec3cca8
Decommission Status : Normal
Configured Capacity: 84415266816 (78.62 GB)
DFS Used: 45056 (44 KB)
Non DFS Used: 27943763968 (26.02 GB)
DFS Remaining: 56471457792 (52.59 GB)
DFS Used%: 0.00%
DFS Remaining%: 66.90%
Configured Cache Capacity: 0 (0 B)
Cache Used: 0 (0 B)
Cache Remaining: 0 (0 B)
Cache Used%: 100.00%
Cache Remaining%: 0.00%
Xceivers: 1
Last contact: Fri Jun 01 05:44:37 UTC 2018

hadoop@d8dbf809c9e0:~/hadoop$
```

2. 运行 wordcount 实例

在 namenode 节点上，执行 hadoop 自带的 wordcount 实例：

```
$ hadoop jar /hadoop/hadoop/share/hadoop/mapreduce/hadoop-mapreduce-examples-2.6.0.jar wordcount /test.txt /test-out
```

```
hadoop@eb108126bc74:~/hadoop$ hadoop jar /hadoop/hadoop/share/hadoop/mapreduce/hadoop-mapreduce-examples-2.6.0.ja
Not a valid JAR: /hadoop/hadoop/share/hadoop/mapreduce/hadoop-mapreduce-examples-2.6.0.ja
hadoop@eb108126bc74:~/hadoop$ hadoop jar /hadoop/hadoop/share/hadoop/mapreduce/hadoop-mapreduce-examples-2.6.0.jar wordcount /test.txt /test-out
18/05/31 06:34:28 INFO client.RMProxy: Connecting to ResourceManager at ha-nn-001/10.42.254.226:8032
18/05/31 06:34:29 INFO input.FileInputFormat: Total input paths to process : 1
18/05/31 06:34:29 INFO mapreduce.JobSubmitter: number of splits:1
18/05/31 06:34:29 INFO mapreduce.JobSubmitter: Submitting tokens for job: job_1527748237836_0002
18/05/31 06:34:30 INFO impl.YarnClientImpl: Submitted application application_1527748237836_0002
18/05/31 06:34:30 INFO mapreduce.Job: The url to track the job: http://ha-nn-001:8088/proxy/application_1527748237836_0002/
18/05/31 06:34:30 INFO mapreduce.Job: Running job: job_1527748237836_0002
18/05/31 06:34:36 INFO mapreduce.Job: Job job_1527748237836_0002 running in uber mode : false
18/05/31 06:34:36 INFO mapreduce.Job:  map 0% reduce 0%
18/05/31 06:34:40 INFO mapreduce.Job:  map 100% reduce 0%
18/05/31 06:34:46 INFO mapreduce.Job:  map 100% reduce 100%
18/05/31 06:34:46 INFO mapreduce.Job: Job job_1527748237836_0002 completed successfully
18/05/31 06:34:46 INFO mapreduce.Job: Counters: 49
        File System Counters
                FILE: Number of bytes read=57
                FILE: Number of bytes written=211307
                FILE: Number of read operations=0
                FILE: Number of large read operations=0
                FILE: Number of write operations=0
```

```
                        Total   vcore-seconds  taken  by  all  reduce   tasks=2977
                        Total   megabyte-seconds  taken  by  all  map   tasks=2631680
                        Total   megabyte-seconds  taken  by  all  reduce   tasks=3048448
        Map-Reduce  Framework
                        Map  input  records=5
                        Map  output  records=7
                        Map  output  bytes=74
                        Map  output  materialized  bytes=57
                        Input  split  bytes=95
                        Combine  input  records=7
                        Combine  output  records=4
                        Reduce  input  groups=4
                        Reduce  shuffle  bytes=57
                        Reduce  input  records=4
                        Reduce  output  records=4
                        Spilled  Records=8
                        Shuffled  Maps =1
                        Failed  Shuffles=0
                        Merged  Map  outputs=1
                        GC  time  elapsed  (ms)=40
                        CPU  time  spent  (ms)=1020
                        Physical  memory  (bytes)  snapshot=548864000
                        Virtual  memory  (bytes)  snapshot=1779597312
                        Total  committed  heap  usage  (bytes)=402653184
        Shuffle  Errors
                        BAD_ID=0
                        CONNECTION=0
                        IO_ERROR=0
                        WRONG_LENGTH=0
                        WRONG_MAP=0
                        WRONG_REDUCE=0
        File  Input  Format  Counters
                        Bytes  Read=48
        File  Output  Format  Counters
                        Bytes  Written=35
hadoop@eb108126bc74:~/hadoop$
```

在 namenode 节点上，查看结果：

$ hadoop fs -ls /

$ hadoop fs -ls /test-out

$ hadoop fs -tail /test-out/part-r-00000

```
hadoop@eb108126bc74:~/hadoop$ hadoop fs -ls /test-out
Found 2 items
-rw-r--r--   3 hadoop supergroup          0 2018-05-31 06:34 /test-out/_SUCCESS
-rw-r--r--   3 hadoop supergroup         35 2018-05-31 06:34 /test-out/part-r-00000
hadoop@eb108126bc74:~/hadoop$ hadoop fs -tail /test-out/part-r-00000
MapReduce       1
hadoop    3
hdfs      2
hive      1
hadoop@eb108126bc74:~/hadoop$
```

至此，hadoop 分布式集群搭建完毕。

第二章 大数据分布式计算框架

实验 2 大数据平台搭建
——MapReduce 进行文本词频统计实验

一、实验介绍

本实验是基于 MapReduce 思想，编写 WordCount 程序。

二、实验原理

1. MapReduce 介绍

MapReduce 是一种计算模型，简单地说就是将大批量的工作（数据）分解（MAP）执行，然后再将结果合并成最终结果（REDUCE）。这样做的好处是在任务被分解后，可以通过大量机器进行并行计算，减少整个操作的时间。

MapReduce 的适用范围：数据量大，但是数据种类少，可以放入内存。

MapReduce 基本原理及要点：将数据交给不同的机器去处理，数据划分，结果归约。

理解 MapReduce 和 YARN：在新版 hadoop 中，YARN 作为一个资源管理调度框架，是 hadoop 下 MapReduce 程序运行的生存环境。其实 MapReduce 除了可以运行在 YARN 框架下，也可以运行在诸如 Mesos、Corona 之类的调度框架上，使用不同的调度框架，需要针对 hadoop 做不同的适配。

一个完整的 MapReduce 程序在 YARN 中执行过程如下。

（1）ResourceManager JobClient 向 ResourceManager 提交一个 job。

（2）ResourceManager 向 Scheduler 请求一个供 MRAppMaster 运行的 container，然后启动它。

（3）MRAppMaster 启动起来后向 ResourceManager 注册。

（4）ResourceManagerJobClient 向 ResourceManager 获取到 MRAppMaster 相关的信息，然后直接与 MRAppMaster 进行通信。

（5）MRAppMaster 算 splits 并为所有的 map 构造资源请求。

（6）MRAppMaster 做一些必要的 MR OutputCommitter 的准备工作。

（7）MRAppMaster 向 RM（Scheduler）发起资源请求，得到一组供 map/reduce task 运行

的 container，然后与 NodeManager 一起对每一个 container 执行一些必要的任务，包括资源本地化等。

（8）MRAppMaster 监视运行着的 task 直到完成；当 task 失败时，申请新的 container 运行失败的 task。

（9）当每个 map/reduce task 完成后，MRAppMaster 运行 MR OutputCommitter 的 cleanup 代码，也就是进行一些收尾工作。

（10）当所有的 map/reduce 完成后，MRAppMaster 运行 OutputCommitter 的必要的 job commit 或者 abort APIs。

（11）MRAppMaster 退出。

2. MapReduce 编程

编写在 hadoop 中依赖 YARN 框架执行的 MapReduce 程序，并不需要自己开发 MRAppMaster 和 YARNRunner，因为 hadoop 已经默认提供通用的 YARNRunner 和 MRAppMaster 程序，大部分情况下只需要编写相应的 Map 处理和 Reduce 处理过程的业务程序即可。

编写一个 MapReduce 程序并不复杂，关键点在于掌握分布式的编程思想和方法，主要将计算过程分为以下 5 个步骤：

（1）迭代。遍历输入数据，并将之解析成 key/value 对。

（2）将输入 key/value 对映射（map）成另外一些 key/value 对。

（3）依据 key 对中间数据进行分组（grouping）。

（4）以组为单位对数据进行归约（reduce）。

（5）迭代。将最终产生的 key/value 对保存到输出文件中。

三、实验要求

实验是基于 hadoop V2.6.0 版本进行，请大家参考前几节 hadoop 的相关安装配置实验进行安装配置。

注意：所有操作都在 hadoop 用户下进行。

四、实验步骤

1. 启动 hadoop 集群并检查

首先启动 hadoop 集群
```
$ su - hadoop
口令输入：hadoop

$ echo $HADOOP_HOME
/hadoop/hadoop
```

上述输出确认 hadoop 的环境变量设置有效,如果无效则激活环境变量:

```
$ bash
$ source ~/.bash_profile
```

启动 ssh,口令输入:hadoop
```
hadoop@ 357987c120a9:~ $ sudo service ssh start
[sudo] password for hadoop:
[ ok ] Starting OpenBSD Secure Shell server: sshd.
```

启动命令:

```
$ start-all.sh
```
检查是否运行成功:
```
# 执行 jps 命令可以查看到 hadoop 的几个主要进程:
$ jps

288 NameNode
528 SecondaryNameNode
367 DataNode
753 NodeManager
1063 Jps
```

2. 上传数据文件到 hdfs

创建/hadoop/hadoop-data/,并进入到/hadoop/hadoop-data/目录下
```
$ mkdir /hadoop/hadoop-data/
$ cd /hadoop/hadoop-data/
```

首先创建一个 test.txt 文件,写入如下内容:

```
$ vi test.txt
hadoop hive hadoop
MapReduce
hdfs hdfs hadoop
```

```
hadoop   hive   hadoop
MapReduce
hdfs    hdfs    hadoop
```

上传至 hdfs：

```
$ hadoop fs -put test.txt /
$ hadoop fs -ls /
```

```
hadoop@299d61e36d41:~/hadoop-data$ hadoop fs -put test.txt /
hadoop@299d61e36d41:~/hadoop-data$ hadoop fs -ls /
Found 2 items
drwxr-xr-x   - hadoop supergroup          0 2018-05-21 06:05 /test
-rw-r--r--   1 hadoop supergroup         48 2018-05-29 01:51 /test.txt
hadoop@299d61e36d41:~/hadoop-data$
```

3. MapReduce 实现 wordcount 实例（Python）

（1）编写 MapReduce WordCount 代码

①编写 map 阶段的代码，创建一个 Python 程序，命名为"count_mapper.py"，使用 vi count_mapper.py 创建该程序，写入如下内容：

```python
#！/usr/bin/env python

import sys
for line in sys.stdin:
    line = line.strip()
    words = line.split()
    for word in words:
        print '%s\t%s' % (word, 1)
```

写入完成后使用如下命令查看该文件中是否写入了上述内容：

```
$ more count_mapper.py
```

②编写 reduce 阶段的代码，创建一个 Python 程序，命名为"count_reducer.py"，使用 vi count_reducer.py 创建该程序，写入如下内容：

```python
#！/usr/bin/env python

from operator import itemgetter
import sys
```

```python
current_word = None
current_count = 0
word = None

for line in sys.stdin:
    line = line.strip()
    word, count= line.split('\t', 1)

    try:
        count = int(count)
    except ValueError:
        continue

    if current_word == word:
        current_count += count
    else:
        if current_word:
            print '% s\t% s' % (current_word, current_count)
        current_count = count
        current_word = word

# do not forget to output the last word if needed!
if current_word == word:
    print '% s\t% s' % (current_word, current_count)
```

写入完成后使用如下命令查看该文件中是否写入了上述内容：

```
$ more count_reducer.py
```

（2）程序编写完成后，首先在本地测试一下 map 和 reduce，命令及图片如下：

```
$ head -3 /hadoop/hadoop-data/test.txt | python count_mapper.py | sort | python count_reducer.py
```

```
hadoop@299d61e36d41:~/hadoop-data$ head -3 /hadoop/hadoop-data/test.txt | python count_mapper.py |
python count_reducer.py
hadoop    2
hive      1
MapReduce 1
hadoop@299d61e36d41:~/hadoop-data$
```

如上图所示,就证明 map 和 reduce 程序编写成功。

(3)运行该实例,命令如下:

```
$ hadoop jar /hadoop/hadoop/share/hadoop/tools/lib/hadoop-streaming-2.6.0.jar -file count_mapper.py -mapper count_mapper.py -file count_reducer.py -reducer count_reducer.py -input /test.txt -output /test-out
```

(4)运行结果。

(5)代码透析。

①map 阶段的代码 count_mapper.py 解析如下：

```python
#! /usr/bin/env python

import sys

# 从标准输入过来的数据
for line in sys.stdin:
    # 将首位的空格去掉
    line = line.strip()
    # 将这一行文本切分成单词(按空格)
    words = line.split()
    # 读一个单词写出一个<单词,1>
    for word in words:
        print '%s\t%s' % (word, 1)
```

②reduce 阶段的代码 count_reducer.py 解析如下：

```python
#! /usr/bin/env python

from operator import itemgetter
import sys

current_word = None
current_count = 0
word = None

# 从标准输入过来的数据
for line in sys.stdin:
    # 去除左右空格
    line = line.strip()

    # 按照tab键进行切分,得到word和次数1
    word, count = line.split('\t', 1)

    # 得到的1是一个字符串,需要类型转化
    try:
```

```
        count = int(count)
except ValueError:
        # 如果不能转化成数字,输入有问题,转到下一行
        Continue

# 如果本次读取的单词和上一次一样,对次数加 1
if current_word = = word:
    current_count + = count
else:
    if current_word:
        # 输出统计结果
        print '% s\t% s' % (current_word, current_count)
    current_count = count
    current_word = word

# do not forget to output the last word if needed!
if current_word = = word:
    print '% s\t% s' % (current_word, current_count)
```

五、实验结果

在 hdfs 上查看结果。

```
$ hadoop fs -ls /
$ hadoop fs -ls /test-out
$ hadoop fs -tail /test-out/part-00000
```

```
hadoop@299d61e36d41:~/hadoop-data$ hadoop fs -ls /
Found 4 items
drwxr-xr-x   - hadoop supergroup          0 2018-05-21 06:05 /test
drwxr-xr-x   - hadoop supergroup          0 2018-05-29 01:55 /test-out
-rw-r--r--   1 hadoop supergroup         48 2018-05-29 01:51 /test.txt
drwx------   - hadoop supergroup          0 2018-05-29 01:55 /tmp
hadoop@299d61e36d41:~/hadoop-data$ hadoop fs -ls /test-out
Found 2 items
-rw-r--r--   1 hadoop supergroup          0 2018-05-29 01:55 /test-out/_SUCCESS
-rw-r--r--   1 hadoop supergroup         35 2018-05-29 01:55 /test-out/part-00000
hadoop@299d61e36d41:~/hadoop-data$ hadoop fs -tail /test-out/part-00000
MapReduce       1
hadoop          3
hdfs            2
hive            1
hadoop@299d61e36d41:~/hadoop-data$
```

六、练习题

请在 hdfs 创建一个文件夹/test1,将文件/hadoop/hadoop/README.txt 上传至 hdfs

的/test1 文件夹下，用 MapReduce 实现对该文件的词频统计，结果输出目录为/test1-out。将你执行的命令和输出的结果粘贴到下面的文本框中。

###输入你的作业代码###

###作业代码结束###

第三章 大数据采集

实验3 大数据信息采集
——使用 Flume 完成用户收视数据的收集

一、实验介绍

1. 实验内容

现在有一个日志文件名称为 web.log.2017-10-13,要求使用 flume 采集该文件数据,并提取文件名称,将采集的数据自动输出到 hdfs 的~/web/2017-10-13 目录下。

2. 实验知识点

(1)阅读 flume 自带的拦截器源码,编写拦截器提取文件名称。
(2)自己在本地创建日志文件 web.log.2017-10-13,使用 flume 采集到 hdfs。

3. 实验环境

hadoop2.6.0
Flume1.6.0

二、实验原理

1. Github 官网示例代码

https://github.com/apache/flume/blob/trunk/flume-ng-core/src/main/java/org/apache/flume/interceptor/RegexExtractorInterceptor.java

2. 实验思路

flume 采集数据的时候在 header 头部添加文件名称。

由于 flume 自带拦截器无法解析 header 内容,需要自定义拦截器提取并解析文件名字作为输出路径。

三、实验要求

(1)在安装 Flume 之前要确保 hadoop 集群正常运行。因此本实验需要在"Flume 环境安装部署"后继续进行操作,必须先完成"Flume 环境安装部署"实验。
(2)本次实验使用的是 Flume1.6.0 版本。
(3)所有操作都在 hadoop 用户下进行操作。

四、实验步骤

1. 实验前准备(namenode 和 datanode1 节点)

本次实验分配到的 IP 地址为:namenode(10.42.250.220)、datanode1(10.42.193.23)、datanode2(10.42.154.8)。每个人分配到的 IP 可能不同。在实验过程中,涉及写 IP 地址的部分,大家要根据自己分配到的 IP 地址,修改 namenode、datanode1 和 datanode2 的相应地址。

查看自己分配到的 IP 地址如下图:

```
namenode(10.42.250.220) datanode1(10.42.193.23) datanode2(10.42.154.8)
```

(1)首先切入到 hadoop 用户并进行如下操作:

```
$ su - hadoop
口令输入:hadoop

$ bash
$ echo $ HADOOP_HOME
/hadoop/hadoop
```

上述输出确认 hadoop 的环境变量设置有效,如果无效则激活环境变量:
```
$ source ~/.bash_profile
```

(2)启动 ssh。

启动 ssh,口令输入:hadoop
```
hadoop@ 357987c120a9:~ $ sudo service ssh start
[sudo] password for hadoop:
[ ok ] Starting OpenBSD Secure Shell server: sshd.
hadoop@ 357987c120a9:~ $
```

(3)修改 hosts 文件。

修改配置文件,口令输入:hadoop
hadoop@ 3778f8dee940:~ $ sudo vi /etc/hosts
[sudo] password for hadoop:

将下列内容添加至 hosts 文件的头部,添加时注意下面两点:
(1)注意将节点对应 IP 更改为自己分配到的 IP 地址。
(2)因为这里我们只用到了 namenode 和 datanode1 节点,所以我们只需要在这两个节点的/etc/hosts 文件里写入这两个节点对应的 IP 即可。

添加内容插入到 hosts 文件的顶部位置:

```
# # hadoop nodes# # #
10.42.250.220 namenode
10.42.193.23 datanode1
# # end hadoop# # #
```

添加完的 hosts 文件内容类似下面的样式:

```
# # hadoop nodes# # #
10.42.250.220 namenode
10.42.193.23 datanode1
# # end hadoop# # #

127.0.0.1       localhost
::1     localhost ip6-localhost ip6-loopback
fe00::0 ip6-localnet
ff00::0 ip6-mcastprefix
ff02::1 ip6-allnodes
ff02::2 ip6-allrouters

10.42.250.220   67576dbc4f7b
```

2. 启动 hadoop(namenode 节点)

启动命令为:
$ start-all.sh

检查是否运行成功
执行 jps 命令可以查看到 hadoop 的几个主要进程：
```
$ jps
Jps
SecondaryNameNode
NodeManager
ResourceManager
NameNode
```

如果出现以上结果，证明 DataNode 可能由于某些原因未成功启动，可以将 hadoop 关掉重启一次：
```
$ stop-all.sh
$ start-all.sh
$ jps
NameNode
Jps
NodeManager
ResourceManager
DataNode
SecondaryNameNode
```

3. 创建目录（namenode 节点）

创建放插件 JAR 的目录
```
$ mkdir -p /hadoop/app/flume/plugins.d/RegexExtractorExtInterceptor/lib
```

创建放插件的依赖 JAR 的目录
```
$ mkdir -p /hadoop/app/flume/plugins.d/RegexExtractorExtInterceptor/libext
```

创建放插件使用到的原生库
```
$ mkdir -p /hadoop/app/flume/plugins.d/RegexExtractorExtInterceptor/native
```

4. 编写拦截器提取文件名称并打包

（1）在 Eclipse 中新建一个 java project 项目"Flume"，再新建一个 Package 包"flume"，然后新建一个 class 为"RegexExtractorExtInterceptor"，并编写代码，示例代码如下：

```
package flume;
```

```
/**
 * Licensed to the Apache Software Foundation (ASF) under one
 * or more contributor license agreements.  See the NOTICE file
 * distributed with this work for additional information
 * regarding copyright ownership.  The ASF licenses this file
 * to you under the Apache License, Version 2.0 (the
 * "License"); you may not use this file except in compliance
 * with the License.  You may obtain a copy of the License at
 *
 *     http://www.apache.org/licenses/LICENSE-2.0
 *
 * Unless required by applicable law or agreed to in writing, software
 * distributed under the License is distributed on an "AS IS" BASIS,
 * WITHOUT WARRANTIES OR CONDITIONS OF ANY KIND, either express or implied.
 * See the License for the specific language governing permissions and
 * limitations under the License.
 */
import java.util.List;
import java.util.Map;
import java.util.regex.Matcher;
import java.util.regex.Pattern;

import org.apache.commons.lang.StringUtils;
import org.apache.flume.Context;
import org.apache.flume.Event;
import org.apache.flume.interceptor.Interceptor;
import org.apache.flume.interceptor.RegexExtractorInterceptorPassThroughSerializer;
import org.apache.flume.interceptor.RegexExtractorInterceptorSerializer;
import org.slf4j.Logger;
import org.slf4j.LoggerFactory;

import com.google.common.base.Charsets;
import com.google.common.base.Preconditions;
import com.google.common.base.Throwables;
import com.google.common.collect.Lists;

//实现拦截器
```

```java
public class RegexExtractorExtInterceptor implements Interceptor {
    //正则字符串和序列化字符串
    static final String REGEX = "regex";
    static final String SERIALIZERS = "serializers";

    //打印日志
    private static final Logger logger = LoggerFactory
        .getLogger(RegexExtractorExtInterceptor.class);

    private final Pattern regex;
    private final List< NameAndSerializer> serializers;


    static final String EXTRACTOR_HEADER = "extractorHeader";
    static final boolean DEFAULT_EXTRACTOR_HEADER = false;
    static final String EXTRACTOR_HEADER_KEY = "extractorHeaderKey";

    private final boolean extractorHeader;
    private final String extractorHeaderKey;

    private RegexExtractorExtInterceptor(Pattern regex,
        List< NameAndSerializer> serializers,boolean extractorHeader,
        String extractorHeaderKey) {
      this.regex = regex;
      this.serializers = serializers;
      this.extractorHeader = extractorHeader;
      this.extractorHeaderKey = extractorHeaderKey;
    }

    public void initialize() {
       // NO-OP...
    }


    public void close() {
       // NO-OP...
    }


    public Event intercept(Event event) {
```

```
    String tmpStr;

    if(extractorHeader)
    {
        tmpStr = event.getHeaders().get(extractorHeaderKey);
    }
    else
    {
        tmpStr= new String(event.getBody(),
            Charsets.UTF_8);
    }

    Matcher matcher = regex.matcher(tmpStr);

Map< String, String> headers = event.getHeaders();
if (matcher.find()) {
  for (int group = 0, count = matcher.groupCount(); group < count; group++ ) {
    int groupIndex = group + 1;
    if (groupIndex > serializers.size()) {
      if (logger.isDebugEnabled()) {
        logger.debug("Skipping group {} to {} due to missing serializer",
            group, count);
      }
      break;
    }
    NameAndSerializer serializer = serializers.get(group);
    if (logger.isDebugEnabled()) {
      logger.debug("Serializing {} using {}", serializer.headerName,
          serializer.serializer);
    }

    headers.put(serializer.headerName,
        serializer.serializer.serialize(matcher.group(groupIndex)));
  }
}
    return event;
}
```

```java
public List< Event> intercept(List< Event> events) {
  List< Event> intercepted = Lists.newArrayListWithCapacity(events.size());
  for (Event event : events) {
    Event interceptedEvent = intercept(event);
    if (interceptedEvent ! = null) {
      intercepted.add(interceptedEvent);
    }
  }
  return intercepted;
}

public static class Builder implements Interceptor.Builder {

  private Pattern regex;
  private List< NameAndSerializer> serializerList;


  private boolean extractorHeader;
  private String extractorHeaderKey;



  private final RegexExtractorInterceptorSerializer defaultSerializer =
      new RegexExtractorInterceptorPassThroughSerializer();

  public void configure(Context context) {
    String regexString = context.getString(REGEX);
    Preconditions.checkArgument(! StringUtils.isEmpty(regexString),
        "Must supply a valid regex string");
    regex = Pattern.compile(regexString);
    regex.pattern();
    regex.matcher("").groupCount();
    configureSerializers(context);

    extractorHeader = context.getBoolean(EXTRACTOR_HEADER,
        DEFAULT_EXTRACTOR_HEADER);

    if (extractorHeader) {
      extractorHeaderKey = context.getString(EXTRACTOR_HEADER_KEY);
```

```java
        Preconditions.checkArgument(
            ! StringUtils.isEmpty(extractorHeaderKey),
            "Must supply header key");
    }

}

private void configureSerializers(Context context) {

  String serializerListStr = context.getString(SERIALIZERS);
  Preconditions.checkArgument(! StringUtils.isEmpty(serializerListStr),
      "Must supply at least one name and serializer");

  String[] serializerNames = serializerListStr.split("\\s+");

  Context serializerContexts =
      new Context(context.getSubProperties(SERIALIZERS + "."));

  serializerList = Lists.newArrayListWithCapacity(serializerNames.length);
  for (String serializerName : serializerNames) {
    Context serializerContext = new Context(
        serializerContexts.getSubProperties(serializerName + "."));
    String type = serializerContext.getString("type", "DEFAULT");
    String name = serializerContext.getString("name");
    Preconditions.checkArgument(! StringUtils.isEmpty(name),
        "Supplied name cannot be empty.");

    if ("DEFAULT".equals(type)) {
      serializerList.add(new NameAndSerializer(name, defaultSerializer));
    } else {
      serializerList.add(new NameAndSerializer(name, getCustomSerializer(
          type, serializerContext)));
    }
  }
}

private RegexExtractorInterceptorSerializer getCustomSerializer(
    String clazzName, Context context) {
  try {
```

```
        RegexExtractorInterceptorSerializer serializer =  (RegexExtractorInterceptor
Serializer) Class
            .forName(clazzName).newInstance();
      serializer.configure(context);
      return serializer;
    } catch (Exception e) {
      logger.error("Could not instantiate event serializer.", e);
      Throwables.propagate(e);
    }
    return defaultSerializer;
  }

  public Interceptor build() {

    Preconditions.checkArgument(regex ! = null,
        "Regex pattern was misconfigured");

    Preconditions.checkArgument(serializerList.size() > 0,
        "Must supply a valid group match id list");

    return new RegexExtractorExtInterceptor (regex, serializerList, extractorHeader,
extractorHeaderKey);
  }
}


  static class NameAndSerializer {
    private final String headerName;
    private final RegexExtractorInterceptorSerializer serializer;

    public NameAndSerializer(String headerName,
        RegexExtractorInterceptorSerializer serializer) {
      this.headerName = headerName;
      this.serializer = serializer;
    }
  }
}
```

(2)在项目中引入hadoop的jar包。

①首先从http://archive.apache.org/dist/flume/1.6.0/apache-flume-1.6.0-bin.tar.gz下载apache-flume-1.6.0-bin.tar.gz到自己电脑并解压。②右键点击工程名→build path→最后一个选项→Libraries→Add Extemal JARS ……③找到刚才解压的文件,并找到目录:/apache-flume-1.6.0-bin/lib,将里面的全部.jar包选中→OK。

(3)将项目打包。

右键点击类"RegexExtractorExtInterceptor.java"→Export..→java→JAR file→JAR file:(写入路径)\Desktop\RegexExtractorExtInterceptor.jar,并选中项目中的.classpath文件和.project文件,如下图所示:

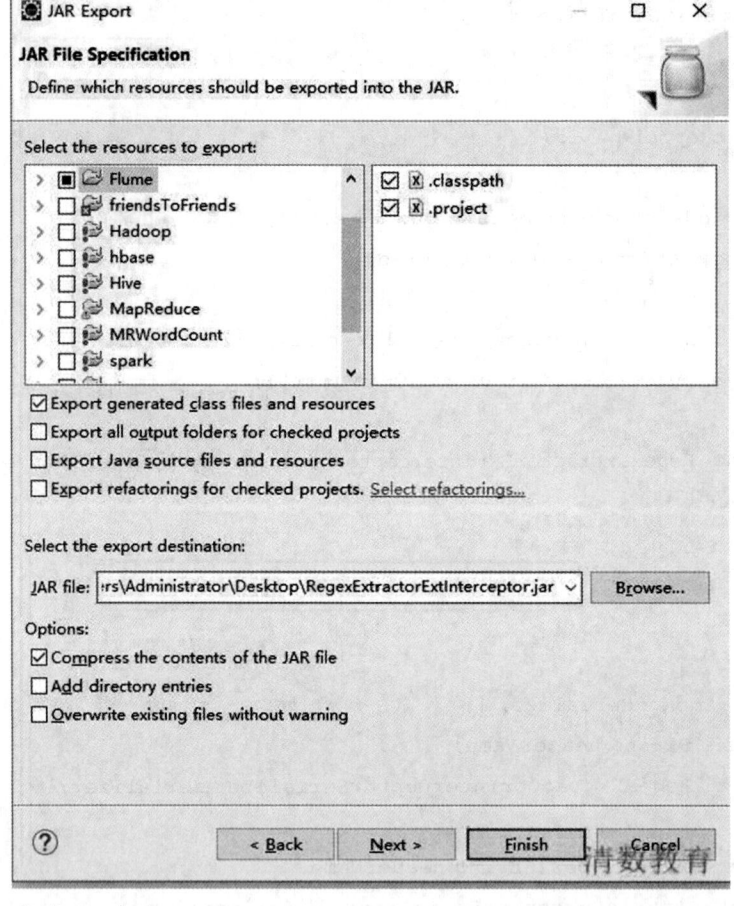

选中Finish完成jar打包。

本次实验程序的jar包:RegexExtractorExtInterceptor.jar,本平台已将其放至共享目录/home/ds/data/tools/下的project/flume-Interceptor目录下,大家直接使用即可。

只要在namenode节点上使用如下命令将RegexExtractorExtInterceptor.jar复制到/hadoop/app/flume/plugins.d/RegexExtractorExtInterceptor/lib下,直接进行步骤5。

```
$ cp /home/ds/data/tools/project/flume-Interceptor/RegexExtractorExtInterceptor.jar /hadoop/app/flume/plugins.d/RegexExtractorExtInterceptor/lib
```

这时候就可以跳过步骤4。

(4)将项目的jar包上传至本实验平台(namenode节点)。

将该jar包上传至本实验平台,上传步骤如下图所示:

首先,点击实验平台左上角的菜单 Menu→File→Open;然后在打开的页面中选择页面右上角的 Upload,选择要上传的文件;最后,在即将上传的文件处选择 Upload 即可。

上传后的文件所在文件夹为:/home/ds/notebooks
```
$ cd /home/ds/notebooks
$ ls -l
```

将其复制到/hadoop/app/flume/plugins.d/RegexExtractorExtInterceptor/lib 目录下
```
$ cp /home/ds/notebooks/RegexExtractorExtInterceptor.jar /hadoop/app/flume/plugins.d/RegexExtractorExtInterceptor/lib
```

5. 写配置文件：flume-conf-Interceptor.properties(namenode 节点)

进入 flume/conf 目录。
```
$ cd /hadoop/app/flume/conf
```

通过 flume-conf.properties.template 复制一个 flume-conf-Interceptor.properties 配置文件。
```
$ cp flume-conf.properties.template flume-conf-Interceptor.properties
```

写配置文件：flume-conf-Interceptor.properties。这里将日志采集到 hdfs 文件系统。配置参数的详细说明可以参考官方文档。
```
$ vi flume-conf-Interceptor.properties
```

找到下面的文字：
```
# The configuration file needs to define the sources,
# the channels and the sinks.
# Sources, channels and sinks are defined per agent,
# in this case called 'agent'
```

将下列内容写入上面的文字下方：
```
# Define source, channel, sink
agent1.sources = spool-source1
agent1.channels = ch1
agent1.sinks = hdfs-sink1

# Define and configure an Spool directory source
agent1.sources.spool-source1.channels = ch1
agent1.sources.spool-source1.type = spooldir
agent1.sources.spool-source1.spoolDir = /hadoop/data/flume/spooldir
agent1.sources.spool-source1.fileHeader= true
agent1.sources.spool-source1.basenameHeader= true
agent1.sources.spool-source1.interceptors= i1
agent1.sources.spool-source1.interceptors.i1.type = flume.RegexExtractorExtInterceptor$Builder
agent1.sources.spool-source1.interceptors.i1.regex= (.*)\\.(.*)\\.(.*)
agent1.sources.spool-source1.interceptors.i1.extractorHeader= true
agent1.sources.spool-source1.interceptors.i1.extractorHeaderKey= basename
agent1.sources.spool-source1.interceptors.i1.serializers= s1 s2 s3
agent1.sources.spool-source1.interceptors.i1.serializers.s1.name= one
```

```
agent1.sources.spool-source1.interceptors.i1.serializers.s2.name= two
agent1.sources.spool-source1.interceptors.i1.serializers.s3.name= three

# Configure channel
agent1.channels.ch1.type =  file
agent1.channels.ch1.checkpointDir =  /hadoop/data/flume/checkpointDir
agent1.channels.ch1.dataDirs =  /hadoop/data/flume/dataDirs

# Define and configure a hdfs sink
agent1.sinks.hdfs-sink1.channel =  ch1
agent1.sinks.hdfs-sink1.type =  hdfs
agent1.sinks.hdfs-sink1.hdfs.path =  hdfs://localhost:9000/flume/%{one}/%{three}
agent1.sinks.hdfs-sink1.hdfs.callTimeout =  20000
```

下面是对该文件的部分说明：

(1) Define source，channel，sink：定义 3 个插件名称。

(2) Define and configure an Spool directory source：使用 spooldir 监控日志目录。

(3) Configure channel：channel 选择 file，防止数据丢失。

(4) Define and configure a hdfs sink：数据采集到 hdfs。

(5) agent1. sources. spool - source1. interceptors. i1. type = flume. RegexExtractor ExtInterceptor $ Builder 这里"flume. RegexExtractorExtInterceptor"的"flume"指的是前面我们编写的拦截器提取文件名称的 java 类的 Package 包名；"RegexExtractorExtInterceptor"指的是前面我们编写的拦截器提取文件名称的 java 类的 Class 类名。

6. 建立相关目录(namenode 节点)

```
$ mkdir -p /hadoop/data/flume/spooldir
$ cd /hadoop/data/flume
$ ls
checkpointDir   dataDirs   spooldir

如果 checkpoint 和 checkpointDir 两个目录存在，则不用执行以下两个创建文件夹的命令：
$ mkdir -p /hadoop/data/flume/checkpointDir
$ mkdir -p /hadoop/data/flume/dataDirs
```

7. 在 namenode 节点上启动 flume

```
$ cd /hadoop/app/flume/
$ bin/flume-ng agent -n agent1 -f conf/flume-conf-Interceptor.properties
```
需要注意的是：-n 指定 agent 的名称;-f 后跟具体的配置文件。

如下图证明启动成功：

```
18/06/29 07:22:11 INFO file.ReplayHandler: Starting replay of [/hadoop/data/flume/dataDirs/log-1]
18/06/29 07:22:11 INFO file.ReplayHandler: Replaying /hadoop/data/flume/dataDirs/log-1
18/06/29 07:22:11 INFO tools.DirectMemoryUtils: Unable to get maxDirectMemory from VM: NoSuchMethod
on: sun.misc.VM.maxDirectMemory(null)
18/06/29 07:22:11 INFO tools.DirectMemoryUtils: Direct Memory Allocation: Allocation = 1048576
= 0, MaxDirectMemorySize = 18874368, Remaining = 18874368
18/06/29 07:22:11 INFO file.LogFile: fast-forward to checkpoint position: 347
18/06/29 07:22:11 INFO file.LogFile: Encountered EOF at 347 in /hadoop/data/flume/dataDirs/log-1
18/06/29 07:22:11 INFO file.ReplayHandler: read: 0, put: 0, take: 0, rollback: 0, commit: 0, sk
tCount:0
18/06/29 07:22:11 INFO file.FlumeEventQueue: Search Count = 0, Search Time = 0, Copy Count
= 0
18/06/29 07:22:11 INFO file.Log: Rolling /hadoop/data/flume/dataDirs
18/06/29 07:22:11 INFO file.Log: Roll start /hadoop/data/flume/dataDirs
18/06/29 07:22:11 INFO file.LogFile: Opened /hadoop/data/flume/dataDirs/log-2
18/06/29 07:22:11 INFO file.Log: Roll end
18/06/29 07:22:11 INFO file.EventQueueBackingStoreFile: Start checkpoint for /hadoop/data/flume/checkp
Dir/checkpoint, elements to sync = 0
18/06/29 07:22:11 INFO file.EventQueueBackingStoreFile: Updating checkpoint metadata: logWriteOrderID
0256931591, queueSize: 0, queueHead: 1
18/06/29 07:22:11 INFO file.Log: Updated checkpoint for file: /hadoop/data/flume/dataDirs/log-2
0 logWriteOrderID: 1530256931591
18/06/29 07:22:11 INFO file.FileChannel: Queue Size after replay: 0 [channel=ch1]
18/06/29 07:22:11 INFO instrumentation.MonitoredCounterGroup: Monitored counter group for type:
ame: ch1: Successfully registered new MBean.
18/06/29 07:22:11 INFO instrumentation.MonitoredCounterGroup: Component type: CHANNEL, name: ch1
18/06/29 07:22:11 INFO node.Application: Starting Sink hdfs-sink1
18/06/29 07:22:11 INFO node.Application: Starting Source spool-source1
18/06/29 07:22:11 INFO source.SpoolDirectorySource: SpoolDirectorySource source starting with dir
hadoop/data/flume/spooldir
18/06/29 07:22:11 INFO instrumentation.MonitoredCounterGroup: Monitored counter group for type:
: hdfs-sink1: Successfully registered new MBean.
18/06/29 07:22:11 INFO instrumentation.MonitoredCounterGroup: Component type: SINK, name: hdfs-sink1
ed
18/06/29 07:22:11 INFO instrumentation.MonitoredCounterGroup: Monitored counter group for type:
me: spool-source1: Successfully registered new MBean.
18/06/29 07:22:11 INFO instrumentation.MonitoredCounterGroup: Component type: SOURCE, name: spool-source
started
```

Sink和Source已经启动
监控的目录

8. datanode1 节点 ssh 远程连接 namenode 节点(datenode1 节点)

ssh 远程连接 namenode 节点时，需要输入 namenode 节点的 hadoop 用户的密码：hadoop
```
$ ssh namenode
```
询问是否确认连接时，输入 yes
```
Are you sure you want to continue connecting (yes/no)? yes
```

```
$ bash
$ echo $HADOOP_HOME
/hadoop/hadoop
```

上述输出确认 hadoop 的环境变量设置有效，如果无效则激活环境变量：

```
$ source ~/.bash_profile
```

9. 在本地新建一个文件 web.log.2017-10-13,上传至监控目录/hadoop/data/flume/spooldir(datenode1 节点)

```
$ cd /hadoop/data/flume/
$ vi web.log.2017-10-13
```

写入如下内容:

```
hadoop
MapReduce
Flume
$ mv web.log.2017-10-13 spooldir
```

五、实验结果

1. 在 namenode 节点上观察 flume 采集数据的日志信息

此时可以看到控制台打印有 flume 采集数据的日志信息。

```
18/06/29 07:22:11 INFO instrumentation.MonitoredCounterGroup: Monitored counter group for type: me: spool-source1: Successfully registered new MBean.
18/06/29 07:22:11 INFO instrumentation.MonitoredCounterGroup: Component type: SOURCE, name: spool started
18/06/29 07:23:21 INFO avro.ReliableSpoolingFileEventReader: Last read took us just up to a f Rolling to the next file, if there is one.
18/06/29 07:23:21 INFO avro.ReliableSpoolingFileEventReader: Preparing to move file /hadoop/data/ oldir/web.log.2017-10-13 to /hadoop/data/flume/spooldir/web.log.2017-10-13.COMPLETED
18/06/29 07:23:21 INFO hdfs.HDFSSequenceFile: writeFormat = Writable, UseRawLocalFileSystem = fa
18/06/29 07:23:21 INFO hdfs.BucketWriter: Creating hdfs://localhost:9000/flume/web/2017-10-13/ 30257001803.tmp
```

2. 在 hdfs 界面查看 flume 采集过来的数据(datanode1 节点)

在 hdfs 界面查看 flume 正在采集数据的过程:

```
$ hadoop fs -ls /flume
$ hadoop fs -ls -R /flume/web
```

如下图所示:

3. 再次在 namenode 节点上观察 flume 采集数据的日志信息

此时可以看到控制台打印有 flume 采集数据成功的日志信息。

4. 再次在 hdfs 界面查看 flume 采集过来的数据（datanode1 节点）

如果看到我们采集的数据，说明 flume 采集数据成功。

```
$ hadoop fs -ls -R /flume/web
```

如下图所示，证明采集成功：

（1）在 namenode 节点按"CTRL＋C"即可结束。

（2）至此一个 flume 的应用场景已经分析完毕，大家可以根据需求完成其他实现方式，详细配置可以查看 flume 官方文档。

实验 4　爬虫实验-大数据信息采集
——使用 Request 进行二手房网站信息爬取和初步分析

一、实验介绍

动手做一个练习，做到学以致用。这次，我们来爬取链家网的一些内容，用的工具依旧是大家熟悉的 requests 和 BeautifulSoup。

二、实验步骤

1. 准备工作

编写爬虫前的准备工作，我们需要导入用到的库，这里主要使用的是 requests 和 BeautifulSoup 两个。还有一个 Time 库，负责设置每次爬取的休息时间。

```
import requests
import time
from bs4 import BeautifulSoup
```

2. 爬取列表页

开始爬取前应该了解一下目标网站 URL 结构。链家网的二手房列表页面共有 100 个，URL 结构为 http://bj.lianjia.com/ershoufang/pg9/ 其中：

(1) bj 表示城市；
(2) /ershoufang/ 是频道名称；
(3) pg9 是页面码。

我们要爬取的是北京的二手房频道，所以前面的部分不会变，属于固定部分，后面的页面码需要在 1~100 间变化，属于可变部分。将 URL 分为两部分，前面的固定部分赋值给 URL，后面的可变部分使用 for 循环遍历页面。

```
# 设置列表页 URL 的固定部分
url= 'http://bj.lianjia.com/ershoufang/'
# 设置页面页的可变部分
page= ('pg')
```

我们最好在 http 请求中设置一个头部信息，否则很容易被封 ip。头部信息网上有很多现成的,也可以使用 httpwatch 等工具来查看。

```
# 设置请求头部信息
headers = {'User-Agent':'Mozilla/5.0 (Windows NT 6.1) AppleWebKit/537.11 (KHTML, like
Gecko) Chrome/23.0.1271.64 Safari/537.11',
'Accept':'text/html;q= 0.9,* /* ;q= 0.8',
'Accept-Charset':'ISO-8859-1,utf-8;q= 0.7,* ;q= 0.3',
'Accept-Encoding':'gzip',
'Connection':'close',
'Referer':'http://www.baidu.com/link? url= _andhfsjjjKRgEWkj7i9cFmYYGsisrnm2A-
TN3XZDQXxvGsM9k9ZZSnikW2Yds4s&amp; amp; wd = &amp; amp; eqid = c3435a7d00146bd60000-
0003582bfd1f'
}
```

我们使用 for 循环生成 1~100 的数字,转化格式后与前面的 URL 固定部分拼成要爬取的 URL。这里我们设置每两个页面间隔 0.5s。爬取到的页面保存在 html 中。

```
# 循环爬取列表页信息
for i in range(1,10):
    if i = = 1:
        i= str(i)
        a= (url+ page+ i+ '/')
        r= requests.get(url= a,headers= headers)
        html= r.content
    else:
        i= str(i)
        a= (url+ page+ i+ '/')
        r= requests.get(url= a,headers= headers)
        html2= r.content
        html = html + html2
    # 每次间隔 3 秒
    time.sleep(3)
```

3. 页面解析

至此,页面爬取的工作就完成了,内容在 html 中,下一步就要进行页面解析了。我们依旧使用 BeautifulSoup 对页面进行解析。

```python
# 解析爬取的页面内容
lj= BeautifulSoup(html,'html.parser')
```

完成页面解析后就可以对页面中的关键信息进行提取了。下面我们分别对房源的总价、房源信息和关注度三部分进行提取。把页面 div 标签中 class＝priceInfo 的部分提取出来，并使用 for 循环将其中每个房源的总价数据存在 tp 中。

```python
# 提取房源总价
price= lj.find_all('div','priceInfo')
tp= []
for a in price:
    totalPrice= a.span.string
    tp.append(totalPrice)
```

来看看爬取出来的房价数据。

```
tp
[u'790',
 u'388',
 u'890',
 u'460',
 u'615',
 u'258',
 u'588',
 u'510',
 u'345',
 ...
```

提取房源信息和关注度的方法与提取房源价格的方法类似，下面是具体的代码，房源信息存储在 hi 中，关注度存储在 fi 中。

```python
# 提取房源信息
houseInfo= lj.find_all('div',attrs= {'class':'houseInfo'})

hi= []
for b in houseInfo:
    house= b.get_text()
    hi.append(house)
```

来看看房源信息。

```
for item in hi:
    print item
```

首城国际 B 区 /2 室 1 厅/88.85m^2/南北/精装/有电梯
金福家园 /2 室 1 厅/78.77m^2/东南北/其他/有电梯
风景 club /3 室 1 厅/124.03m^2/南北/精装/有电梯
天通苑北一区 /2 室 1 厅/112.74m^2/东南/精装/有电梯
新龙城 /3 室 1 厅/113.19m^2/南北/精装/有电梯
御景春天 /1 室 1 厅/48.42m^2/东/简装/有电梯
玉海园五里 /2 室 1 厅/80.39m^2/东 西/简装/无电梯
新街坊 /2 室 1 厅/92.64m^2/西/精装/有电梯
……

```
# 提取房源关注度
followInfo= lj.find_all('div',attrs= {'class':'followInfo'})

fi= []
for c in followInfo:
    follow= c.get_text()
fi.append(follow)
```

再来看看关注度状况。

```
for item in fi:
    print item
```

2718 人关注/55 次带看近地铁房本满五年随时看房 790 万元单价 88 914 元/m^2
650 人关注/46 次带看房本满五年随时看房 388 万元单价 49 258 元/m^2
3876 人关注/44 次带看近地铁房本满五年随时看房 890 万元单价 71 757 元/m^2
6660 人关注/41 次带看近地铁房本满五年随时看房 460 万元单价 40 802 元/m^2
14 371 人关注/46 次带看近地铁房本满五年随时看房 615 万元单价 54 334 元/m^2
353 人关注/43 次带看近地铁房本满五年随时看房 258 万元单价 53 284 元/m^2
243 人关注/20 次带看房本满五年随时看房 588 万元单价 73 144 元/m^2
922 人关注/39 次带看近地铁房本满五年随时看房 510 万元单价 55 052 元/m^2
122 人关注/36 次带看房本满五年随时看房 345 万元单价 38 852 元/m^2
1007 人关注/85 次带看近地铁房本满五年随时看房 469 万元单价 46 358 元/m^2

307 人关注/39 次带看近地铁房本满五年随时看房 800 万元单价 83 282 元/m²
784 人关注/67 次带看房本满五年随时看房 290 万元单价 28 776 元/m²
90 人关注/38 次带看近地铁房本满五年随时看房 780 万元单价 73 718 元/m²
190 人关注/44 次带看近地铁房本满五年随时看房 680 万元单价 65 733 元/m²
288 人关注/42 次带看近地铁房本满五年随时看房 450 万元单价 44 915 元/m²
2462 人关注/31 次带看近地铁房本满五年随时看房 1088 万元单价 80 779 元/m²
685 人关注/54 次带看近地铁房本满五年随时看房 630 万元单价 98 762 元/m²
3272 人关注/16 次带看房本满五年随时看房 810 万元单价 72 142 元/m²
……

4. 清洗数据并整理到数据表中

我们将之前爬取到的信息进行汇总,并导入 pandas 之中生成数据表(表 3-1)。便于后面的分析。

```
# 导入pandas库
import pandas as pd
# 创建数据表
house= pd.DataFrame({'totalprice':tp,'houseinfo':hi,'followinfo':fi})
# 查看数据表的内容
house.head()
```

表 3-1 房源信息

	followinfo	houseinfo	totalprice
0	2718 人关注/55 次带看近地铁房本满五年随时看房 790 万元单价 88 914 元/m²	首城国际 B 区 /2 室 1 厅/88.85m²/南北/精装/有电梯	790
1	650 人关注/46 次带看房本满五年随时看房 388 万元单价 49 258 元/m²	金福家园 /2 室 1 厅/78.77m²/东南北/其他/有电梯	388
2	3876 人关注/44 次带看近地铁房本满五年随时看房 890 万元单价 71 757 元/m²	风景 club /3 室 1 厅/124.03m²/南北/精装/有电梯	890
3	6660 人关注/41 次带看近地铁房本满五年随时看房 460 万元单价 40 802 元/m²	天通苑北一区 /2 室 1 厅/112.74m²/东南/精装/有电梯	460
4	14 371 人关注/46 次带看近地铁房本满五年随时看房 615 万元单价 54 334 元/m²	新龙城 /3 室 1 厅/113.19m²/南北/精装/有电梯	615

尴尬的是,大家看得到,很多信息是连在一起的,不能直接使用,所以我们再做一些数据提取和清洗的工作。如房源信息,在表中每个房源的小区名称、户型、面积、朝向等信息都在一个字段中,无法直接使用。需要先进行分列操作。这里的规则比较明显,每个信息间都是以竖线分割的,因此我们只需要以竖线进行分列即可。

```
# 对房源信息进行分列
houseinfo_split = pd.DataFrame((x.split('|') for x in house.houseinfo),index= house.index,columns= ['xiaoqu','huxing','mianji','chaoxiang','zhuangxiu','dianti'])
```

AssertionErrorTraceback (most recent call last)
< ipython-input-14-6ac0934bfcc5> in < module> ()
    1 # 对房源信息进行分列
----> 2 houseinfo_split = pd.DataFrame((x.split('|') for x in house.houseinfo),index= house.index,columns= ['xiaoqu','huxing','mianji','chaoxiang','zhuangxiu','dianti'])

/opt/conda/envs/python2/lib/python2.7/site-packages/pandas/core/frame.pyc in __init__(self, data, index, columns, dtype, copy)
    303   if is_named_tuple(data[0]) and columns is None:
    304   columns = data[0]._fields
--> 305   arrays, columns = _to_arrays(data, columns, dtype= dtype)
    306   columns = _ensure_index(columns)
    307

/opt/conda/envs/python2/lib/python2.7/site-packages/pandas/core/frame.pyc in _to_arrays(data, columns, coerce_float, dtype)
   5517   if isinstance(data[0], (list, tuple)):
   5518   return _list_to_arrays(data, columns, coerce_float= coerce_float,
-> 5519   dtype= dtype)
   5520   elif isinstance(data[0], collections.Mapping):
   5521   return _list_of_dict_to_arrays(data, columns,

/opt/conda/envs/python2/lib/python2.7/site-packages/pandas/core/frame.pyc in _list_to_arrays(data, columns, coerce_float, dtype)
   5596   content = list(lib.to_object_array(data).T)
   5597 return _convert_object_array(content, columns, dtype= dtype,
-> 5598   coerce_float= coerce_float)
   5599
   5600

/opt/conda/envs/python2/lib/python2.7/site-packages/pandas/core/frame.pyc in _convert_object_array(content,columns, coerce_float, dtype)
   5655   # caller's responsibility to check for this...
   5656   raise AssertionError('% d columns passed, passed data had % s '

```
-> 5657                              'columns' % (len(columns), len(content)))
   5658
   5659          # provide soft conversion of object dtypes

AssertionError: 6 columns passed, passed data had 1 columns
```

现在再来看看我们整理好的数据。

```
# 查看分列结果
houseinfo_split.head()
```

表 3-2 分列结果

	xiaoqu	huxing	mianji	chaoxiang	zhuangxiu	dianti
0	首开知语城	3室2厅	151.39m²	南北	精装	None
1	疃里新村	3室1厅	104.96m²	南北	简装	None
2	天时名苑	2室2厅	121.3m²	南北	精装	有电梯
3	恋日嘉园一期	5室2厅	283.1m²	南北	精装	None
4	美林湾	2室2厅	91.26m²	南北	精装	None

把拆分后的数据拼接回原始数据中。

```
# 将分列结果拼接回原数据表
house= pd.merge(house,houseinfo_split,right_index= True, left_index= True)
```

```
house.head()
```

表 3-3 拼接结果

	follow info	house info	total price	xiaoqu	huxing	mianji	chaoxiang	zhuangxiu	dianti
0	283人关注／共38次带看／19天以前发布	首开知语城｜3室2厅｜151.39m²｜南北｜精装	1515	首开知语城	3室2厅	151.39m²	南北	精装	None

续表 3-3

	follow info	house info	total price	xiao qu	hu xing	mian ji	chao xiang	zhuang xiu	dian ti
1	159人关注／共28次带看／6天以前发布	瞳里新村｜3室1厅｜104.96m²｜南北｜简装	435	瞳里新村	3室1厅	104.96m²	南北	简装	None
2	538人关注／共64次带看／17天以前发布	天时名苑｜2室2厅｜121.3m²｜南北｜精装｜有电梯	695	天时名苑	2室2厅	121.3m²	南北	精装	有电梯
3	135人关注／共35次带看／28天以前发布	恋日嘉园一期｜5室2厅｜283.1m²｜南北｜精装	1850	恋日嘉园一期	5室2厅	283.1m²	南北	精装	None
4	68人关注／共39次带看／6天以前发布	美林湾｜2室2厅｜91.26m²｜南北｜精装	330	美林湾	2室2厅	91.26m²	南北	精装	None

使用相同的方法对房源关注度字段进行分列和拼接操作。这里的分列规则是斜杠。

```
# 对房源关注度进行分列
followinfo_split = pd.DataFrame((x.split('/') for x in house.followinfo),index=
house.index,columns= ['guanzhu','daikan','fabu'])
# 将分列后的关注度信息拼接回原数据表
house= pd.merge(house,followinfo_split,right_index= True, left_index= True)
```

```
house.head()
```

表 3-4 房源关注度信息

	follow info	house info	total price	xiao qu	hu xing	mian ji	chao xiang	zhuang xiu	dianti	guan zhu	dai kan	fabu
0	283人关注 / 共38次带看 / 19天以前发布	首开知语城 | 3室2厅 | 151.39m² | 南北 | 精装	1515	首开知语城	3室2厅	151.39 m²	南北	精装	None	283人关注	共38次带看	19天以前发布
1	159人关注 / 共28次带看 / 6天以前发布	瞳里新村 | 3室1厅 | 104.96m² | 南北 | 简装	435	瞳里新村	3室1厅	104.96 m²	南北	简装	None	159人关注	共28次带看	6天以前发布
2	538人关注 / 共64次带看 / 17天以前发布	天时名苑 | 2室2厅 | 121.3m² | 南北 | 精装 | 有电梯	695	天时名苑	2室2厅	121.3 m²	南北	精装	有电梯	538人关注	共64次带看	17天以前发布
3	135人关注 / 共35次带看 / 28天以前发布	恋日嘉园一期 | 5室2厅 | 283.1m² | 南北 | 精装	1850	恋日嘉园一期	5室2厅	283.1 m²	南北	精装	None	135人关注	共35次带看	28天以前发布
4	68人关注 / 共39次带看 / 6天以前发布	美林湾 | 2室2厅 | 91.26m² | 南北 | 精装	330	美林湾	2室2厅	91.26 m²	南北	精装	None	68人关注	共39次带看	6天以前发布

第四章 大数据管理

实验 5 大数据的预处理
——收视数据的小文件合并实验

一、实验介绍

1. 实验背景

在实际项目中,输入数据往往是由许多小文件组成,这里的小文件是指小于 hdfs 系统 Block 大小的文件(默认 128M),然而每一个存储在 hdfs 中的文件、目录和块都映射为一个对象,存储在 NameNode 服务器内存中,通常占用 150 个字节。如果有一千万个文件,就需要消耗大约 3G 的内存空间。如果是十亿个文件呢,简直不可想象。所以我们要了解一下 hadoop 处理小文件的各种方案,然后选择一种适合的方案来解决本项目的小文件问题。

2. 数据集介绍

该数据集我们已经放在了共享目录/home/ds/data/tools/下的 project/hdfs-data/data 目录下,该目录下有 2012-09-17 至 2012-09-23 一共 7 天的数据集,如下图所示:

```
hadoop@2753234681ab:/home/ds/data/tools/project/hdfs-data/data$ ls -l
total 28
drwxr-xr-x 2 root root 4096 Jun  5 10:00 2012-09-17
drwxr-xr-x 2 root root 4096 Jun  5 10:00 2012-09-18
drwxr-xr-x 2 root root 4096 Jun  5 10:00 2012-09-19
drwxr-xr-x 2 root root 4096 Jun  5 10:01 2012-09-20
drwxr-xr-x 2 root root 4096 Jun  5 10:01 2012-09-21
drwxr-xr-x 2 root root 4096 Jun  5 10:01 2012-09-22
drwxr-xr-x 2 root root 4096 Jun  5 10:01 2012-09-23
hadoop@2753234681ab:/home/ds/data/tools/project/hdfs-data/data$
```

```
drwxr-xr-x  2 root root    4096 Jun  5 10:01 2012-09-22
drwxr-xr-x  2 root root    4096 Jun  5 10:01 2012-09-23
hadoop@2753234681ab:/home/ds/data/tools/project/hdfs-data/data$ cd 2012-09-17/
hadoop@2753234681ab:/home/ds/data/tools/project/hdfs-data/data/2012-09-17$ ls -l
total 14692
-rw-r--r--  1 root root 1111961 Jun  5 09:59 ars10767@20120917000000.txt
-rw-r--r--  1 root root  782533 Jun  5 09:59 ars10767@20120917001500.txt
-rw-r--r--  1 root root  593507 Jun  5 09:59 ars10767@20120917004500.txt
-rw-r--r--  1 root root  839019 Jun  5 09:59 ars10767@20120917010000.txt
-rw-r--r--  1 root root  866393 Jun  5 09:59 ars10767@20120917011500.txt
-rw-r--r--  1 root root  678491 Jun  5 09:59 ars10767@20120917013000.txt
-rw-r--r--  1 root root  593292 Jun  5 09:59 ars10767@20120917014500.txt
-rw-r--r--  1 root root  688620 Jun  5 09:59 ars10767@20120917020000.txt
-rw-r--r--  1 root root  674864 Jun  5 09:59 ars10767@20120917021500.txt
-rw-r--r--  1 root root  635052 Jun  5 09:59 ars10767@20120917023000.txt
-rw-r--r--  1 root root  547324 Jun  5 09:59 ars10767@20120917022500.txt
-rw-r--r--  1 root root  598814 Jun  5 09:59 ars10767@20120917024500.txt
-rw-r--r--  1 root root  542600 Jun  5 09:59 ars10767@20120917030000.txt
-rw-r--r--  1 root root  535446 Jun  5 09:59 ars10767@20120917031500.txt
-rw-r--r--  1 root root  592780 Jun  5 09:59 ars10767@20120917033000.txt
-rw-r--r--  1 root root  619410 Jun  5 09:59 ars10767@20120917034500.txt
-rw-r--r--  1 root root  590326 Jun  5 09:59 ars10767@20120917040000.txt
-rw-r--r--  1 root root  428487 Jun  5 09:59 ars10767@20120917041500.txt
-rw-r--r--  1 root root  598048 Jun  5 09:59 ars10767@20120917043000.txt
-rw-r--r--  1 root root  598792 Jun  5 09:59 ars10767@20120917044500.txt
-rw-r--r--  1 root root  575613 Jun  5 09:59 ars10767@20120917050000.txt
-rw-r--r--  1 root root  619080 Jun  5 10:00 ars10767@20120917051500.txt
-rw-r--r--  1 root root  587763 Jun  5 10:00 ars10767@20120917053000.txt
hadoop@2753234681ab:/home/ds/data/tools/project/hdfs-data/data/2012-09-17$
```

我们需要将这 7 天的数据集按日期合并为 7 个大文件上传至 hdfs。

二、实验原理

项目思路：

(1) 首先通过 globStatus() 方法过滤掉 svn 格式的文件，获取 data 目录下的其他所有文件路径。

(2) 然后循环第一步的所有文件路径，通过 globStatus() 方法获取所有 txt 格式文件路径。

(3) 最后通过 IOUtils.copyBytes(in, out, 4096, false) 方法将数据集合并为 7 个大文件，并上传至 hdfs。

三、实验要求

(1) 本实验需要按照"hadoop：伪分布式集群安装和启动配置"部署后继续进行操作，因此必须先完成"hadoop：伪分布式集群安装和启动配置"实验。

(2) 本实验平台是基于 1.7 版本的 java，请注意 java 的版本统一。

(3) 所有操作都在 hadoop 用户下进行操作。

四、实验步骤

1. 实验前准备

```
$ su - hadoop
```

口令输入:hadoop

```
$ echo $ HADOOP_HOME
/hadoop/hadoop
```

上述输出确认hadoop的环境变量设置有效,如果无效则激活环境变量:
```
$ bash
$ source ~ /.bash_profile
```

启动ssh,口令输入:hadoop
```
hadoop@ 357987c120a9:~ $ sudo service ssh start
[sudo] password for hadoop:
[ ok ] Starting OpenBSD Secure Shell server: sshd.
```

2. 启动 hadoop

启动命令为:
```
$ start-all.sh
```

检查是否运行成功
执行jps命令可以查看到hadoop的几个主要进程:
```
$ jps

288 NameNode
528 SecondaryNameNode
367 DataNode
753 NodeManager
1063 Jps
```

3. 将数据集复制到/hadoop/hadoop-project 目录下

新建文件夹将该项目的数据集移动到该目录下:
```
$ mkdir /hadoop/hadoop-project
$ cd /home/ds/data/tools/project/hdfs-data
$ cp -r data /hadoop/hadoop-project
```

4. 编写 MapReduce 作业

1) 编写项目程序参考步骤

第一步：首先自定义 RegexExcludePathFilter 类实现 PathFilter，通过 accept 方法过滤掉 data 目录下的 svn 文件。

第二步：自定义 RegexAcceptPathFilter 类实现 PathFilter，比如只接受 data\2012-09-17 日期目录下 txt 格式的文件。

第三步：实现主程序 list 方法，完成数据集的合并，并上传至 hdfs。

2) 下面我们来使用 eclipse 工具编写 MapReduce 作业

（1）在 Eclipse 中新建一个 java project 项目"MapReduce"，再新建一个 Package 包 "hadoop.test"，接下来新建一个 class 为"hdfs"，最后编写 MapReduce 代码，MapReduce 示例代码如下：

```java
package hadoop.test;

import java.io.IOException;
import java.net.URI;
import java.net.URISyntaxException;

import org.apache.hadoop.conf.Configuration;
import org.apache.hadoop.fs.FSDataInputStream;
import org.apache.hadoop.fs.FSDataOutputStream;
import org.apache.hadoop.fs.FileStatus;
import org.apache.hadoop.fs.FileSystem;
import org.apache.hadoop.fs.FileUtil;
import org.apache.hadoop.fs.Path;
import org.apache.hadoop.fs.PathFilter;
import org.apache.hadoop.io.IOUtils;

public class hdfs {
    private static FileSystem fs = null;
    private static FileSystem local = null;
    public static void main(String[] args) throws IOException, URISyntaxException {
        list();
    }
    public static void list() throws IOException, URISyntaxException {
        //读取hadoop文件系统的配置
```

```java
Configuration conf = new Configuration();
//文件系统访问接口
URI uri = new URI("hdfs://localhost:9000");
//创建 FileSystem 对象
fs = FileSystem.get(uri, conf);

//获得本地文件系统
local = FileSystem.getLocal(conf);

//过滤目录下的 svn 文件,globStatus 从第一个参数通配符合到文件,剔除满足第二个参
数到结果,因为 PathFilter 中 accept 是 return!
    FileStatus[] dirstatus = local.globStatus(new Path("/hadoop/hadoop-project/data/*"),new RegexExcludePathFilter("^.* svn$"));
//获取 data 目录下的所有文件路径,注意 FIleUtil 中 stat2Paths()的使用,它将一个
FileStatus 对象数组转换为 Path 对象数组。
Path[] dirs = FileUtil.stat2Paths(dirstatus);

FSDataOutputStream out = null;
FSDataInputStream in = null;

for (Path dir : dirs) {
    String fileName = dir.getName().replace("-", "");//文件名称
    //只接受日期目录下的.txt 文件,^匹配输入字符串的开始位置,$ 匹配输入字符串的
结束位置,* 匹配 0 个或多个字符。
    FileStatus[] localStatus = local.globStatus(new Path(dir+ "/*"),new RegexAcceptPathFilter("^.* txt$"));
    //获得日期目录下的所有文件
    Path[] listedPaths = FileUtil.stat2Paths(localStatus);
    //输出路径
    Path block = new Path("hdfs://localhost:9000/hdfs/"+ fileName + ".txt");
    //打开输出流
    out = fs.create(block);
    for (Path p : listedPaths) {
        in = local.open(p);//打开输入流
        //复制数据,IOUtils.copyBytes 可以方便地将数据写入到文件,不需要自己去
控制缓冲区,也不用自己去循环读取输入源。false 表示不自动关闭数据流,那么就手动关闭。
        IOUtils.copyBytes(in, out, 4096, false);
```

```java
                //关闭输入流
                in.close();
            }
            if (out ! = null) {
                //关闭输出流
                out.close();
            }
        }
    }
    /* *
     *
     * @ function 过滤 regex 格式的文件
     *
     * /
    public static class RegexExcludePathFilter implements PathFilter {
        private final String regex;

public RegexExcludePathFilter(String regex) {
            this.regex = regex;
        }
        @ Override
        public boolean accept(Path path) {
            // TODO Auto-generated method stub
            boolean flag = path.toString().matches(regex);
          return ! flag;
        }


    }
    /* *
     *
     * @ function 接受 regex 格式的文件
     *
     * /
    public static class RegexAcceptPathFilter implements PathFilter {
        private final String regex;

        public RegexAcceptPathFilter(String regex) {
            this.regex = regex;
```

```
        }
    @ Override
    public boolean accept(Path path) {
        // TODO Auto-generated method stub
        boolean flag = path.toString().matches(regex);
        return flag;
    }

}
```

(2)在项目中引入hadoop的jar包。

①首先从 https://archive.apache.org/dist/hadoop/common/hadoop-2.6.0/下载hadoop-2.6.0.tar.gz到客户端并解压。②右键点击工程名→bulid path→最后一个选项→Libraries→Add Extemal JARS...③找到刚才解压的文件,并找到目录:/hadoop-2.6.0/share/hadoop,将下面的common、hdfs、mapreduce、YARN 里面的全部.jar包选中→OK,继续Add Extamal→common、hdfs、mapreduce、YARN 这4个文件下的lib的目录下的所有的jar包全选→OK。

(3)将项目打包。

右键点击项目→Export..→java→JAR file→JAR file:(写入路径)\Desktop\hdfs.jar,并选中项目中的.classpath文件和.project文件,如下图所示:

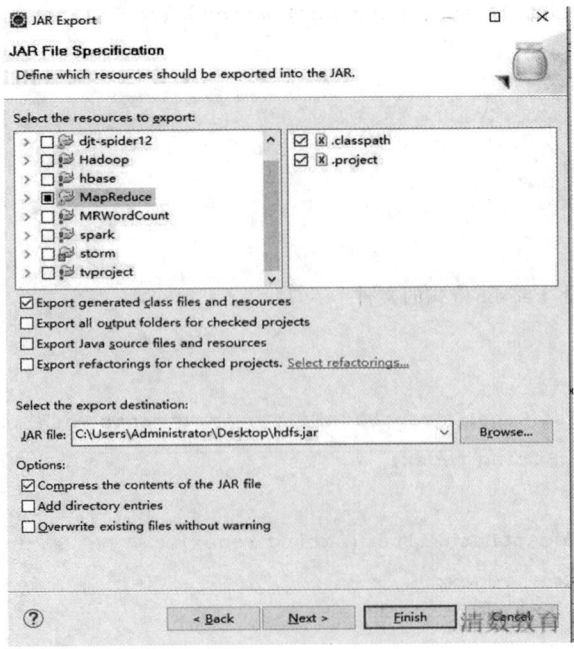

第四章 大数据管理

选中 Finish 完成打 jar 包。

本次实验的 MapReduce 程序的 jar 包:hdfs.jar,已放至本平台共享目录/home/ds/data/tools/下的 project/hdfs-data 目录下,直接使用即可。

使用如下命令,将 hdfs.jar 复制到/hadoop/hadoop-project 下,直接进行步骤 5:

```
$ cp /home/ds/data/tools/project/hdfs-data/hdfs.jar /hadoop/hadoop-project
```

(4)将项目的 jar 包上传至本实验平台。

将该 jar 包上传至本实验平台,上传步骤如下图所示:

首先点击实验平台左上角的菜单 Menu→File→Open,然后在打开的新页面中选择页面右上角的 Upload,选择要上传的文件,最后在即将上传的文件处选择 Upload 即可。

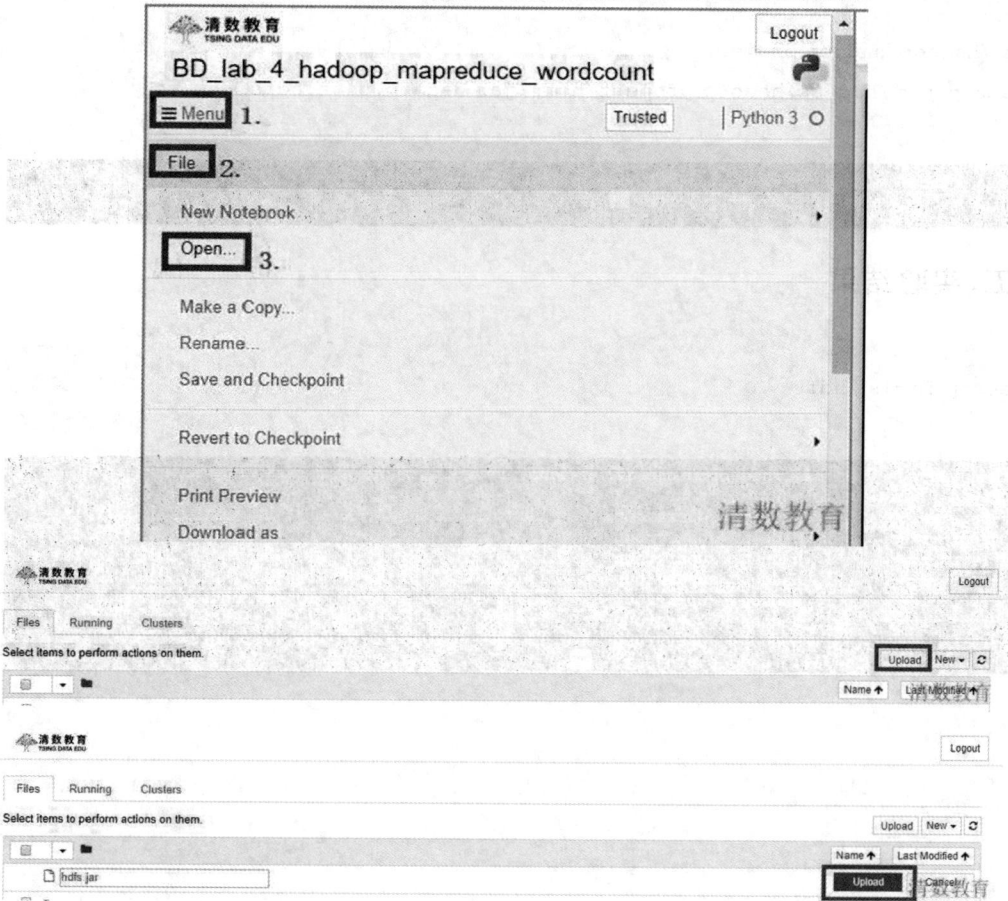

上传后的文件所在文件夹为:/home/ds/notebooks

```
$ cd /home/ds/notebooks
$ ls -l
```

将其复制到/hadoop/hadoop-project目录下
$ cp /home/ds/notebooks/hdfs.jar /hadoop/hadoop-project
$ cd /hadoop/hadoop-project
$ ls -l

```
hadoop@bceae0a3d0e4:/home/ds/notebooks$ cp /home/ds/notebooks/hdfs.jar /hadoop/hadoop-project
hadoop@bceae0a3d0e4:/home/ds/notebooks$ cd /hadoop/hadoop-project
hadoop@bceae0a3d0e4:/hadoop-project$ ls -l
total 12
drwxr-xr-x 9 hadoop hadoop 4096 Jun  5 10:41 data
-rw-r--r-- 1 hadoop hadoop 5330 Jun  5 10:47 hdfs.jar
hadoop@bceae0a3d0e4:/hadoop-project$
```

5. 运行该实例

$ cd /hadoop/hadoop-project
$ hadoop jar /hadoop/hadoop-project/hdfs.jar hadoop.test.hdfs

```
hadoop@bceae0a3d0e4:/hadoop-project$ hadoop jar /hadoop/hadoop-project/hdfs.jar hadoop.test.hdfs
hadoop@bceae0a3d0e4:/hadoop-project$
```

五、实验结果

$ hadoop fs -ls /hdfs

```
hadoop@bceae0a3d0e4:/hadoop-project$ hadoop fs -ls /hdfs
Found 7 items
-rw-r--r--   1 hadoop supergroup   14898215 2018-06-05 10:43 /hdfs/20120917.txt
-rw-r--r--   1 hadoop supergroup   42960042 2018-06-05 10:43 /hdfs/20120918.txt
-rw-r--r--   1 hadoop supergroup   16759738 2018-06-05 10:43 /hdfs/20120919.txt
-rw-r--r--   1 hadoop supergroup   23659691 2018-06-05 10:43 /hdfs/20120920.txt
-rw-r--r--   1 hadoop supergroup   33371348 2018-06-05 10:43 /hdfs/20120921.txt
-rw-r--r--   1 hadoop supergroup   14746702 2018-06-05 10:43 /hdfs/20120922.txt
-rw-r--r--   1 hadoop supergroup   16684000 2018-06-05 10:43 /hdfs/20120923.txt
hadoop@bceae0a3d0e4:/hadoop-project$
```

实验 6 大数据的预处理
——编写 MR 程序对原始的收视数据进行清洗与预处理实验

一、实验介绍

1. 实验内容

很多视频网站都有电视剧热度排名,该排名一般是依据用户在视频网的行为数据所体现出的受欢迎程度来排名。这里有一份来自优酷、爱奇艺、搜狐视频等五大视频网站的视频播放数据,我们可以利用这份数据做些有意义的事情。

注意:1~5 数字和 5 大视频的关系:1 代表优酷;2 代表搜狐;3 代表土豆;4 代表爱奇艺;5 代表迅雷看看。

2. 实验需求

输入数据:5 个网站的每天电视剧的播放量、收藏数、评论数、踩数、赞数。
输出数据:按网站类别统计每个电视剧的每个指标的总量。
任务目标:自定义输入格式、完成统计任务、输出多个文件。

3. 数据集

该数据集我们已经放在了共享目录/home/ds/data/tools/下的 project/tvplay 目录下,即 tvplay.txt。数据集中部分内容如下图所示:

二、实验原理

实验思路和步骤
第一步:定义一个电视剧热度数据的 bean。
第二步:定义一个读取热度数据的 InputFormat 类。

第三步：写 MapReduce 统计程序。
第四步：上传 tvplay.txt 数据集到 hdfs,并运行程序。

三、实验要求

本实验是基于 hadoop V2.6.0 版本,请大家参考前几节 hadoop 的相关安装配置实验进行安装配置。

本实验平台是基于 1.7 版本的 java,请注意 java 的版本统一。

注意：所有操作都在 hadoop 用户下进行操作。

四、实验步骤

1. 实验前准备

```
$ su - hadoop
口令输入:hadoop

$ echo $HADOOP_HOME
/hadoop/hadoop
```

上述输出确认 hadoop 的环境变量设置有效,如果无效则激活环境变量：

```
$ bash
$ source ~/.bash_profile
```

启动 ssh,口令输入:hadoop

```
hadoop@357987c120a9:~$ sudo service ssh start
[sudo] password for hadoop:
[ ok ] Starting OpenBSD Secure Shell server: sshd.
```

2. 启动 hadoop

启动命令为：

```
$ start-all.sh
```

检查是否运行成功
执行 jps 命令可以查看到 hadoop 的几个主要进程：
```
$ jps
```

```
288 NameNode
528 SecondaryNameNode
367 DataNode
753 NodeManager
1063 Jps
```

3. 将数据集上传至 hdfs

新建一个文件夹,将该项目的数据集移动到该目录下:

```
$ mkdir /hadoop/tvplay
$ cd /home/ds/data/tools/project/tvplay/
```

查看文件的前 20 行:

```
$ head -20 tvplay.txt
```

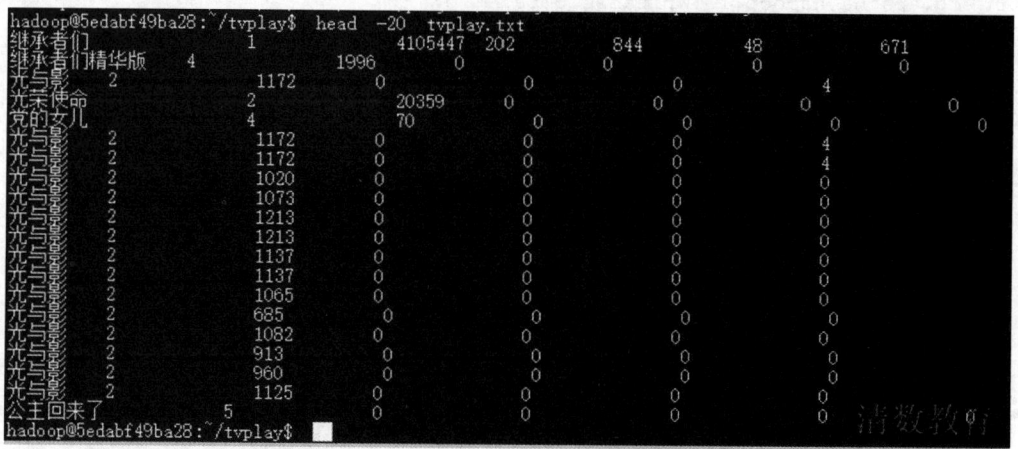

将该文件复制到/hadoop/tvplay 目录下:

```
$ cp  tvplay.txt /hadoop/tvplay
$ cd /hadoop/tvplay
```

将数据集上传至 hdfs:

```
$ hadoop fs -mkdir /tvplay
$ hadoop fs -put /hadoop/tvplay/tvplay.txt /tvplay
$ hadoop fs -ls -R  /tvplay
```

4. 使用 eclipse 工具编写 MapReduce 作业

1）在 Eclipse 中新建一个 java project 项目"MapReduce"，再新建一个 Package 包"hadoop.tv"，接下来编写代码，示例代码如下：

（1）然后新建一个 class 为"TVWritable"。

利用 WritableComparable 接口，自定义一个 TVWritable 类，实现 WritableComparable 类，将各个参数封装起来，便于计算。

```java
package hadoop.tv;

import java.io.DataInput;
import java.io.DataOutput;
import java.io.IOException;

import org.apache.hadoop.io.WritableComparable;

public class TvPlayWritable implements WritableComparable<Object> {

    //定义5个成员变量
    private int daynumber;
    private int collectnumber;
    private int commentnumber;
    private int againstnumber;
    private int supportnumber;

    //构造函数
    public TvPlayWritable(){}

    //定义一个set方法，用this关键字对封装好的数据进行引用
    public void set (int daynumber, int collectnumber, int commentnumber, int againstnumber,int supportnumber){
        this.daynumber = daynumber;
        this.collectnumber = collectnumber;
        this.commentnumber = commentnumber;
```

```java
        this.againstnumber = againstnumber;
        this.supportnumber = supportnumber;
    }

    //使用 get 和 set 对封装好的数据进行存取
    public int getDaynumber() {
        return daynumber;
    }
    public void setDaynumber(int daynumber) {
        this.daynumber = daynumber;
    }

    public int getCollectnumber() {
        return collectnumber;
}
    public void setCollectnumber(int collectnumber) {
        this.collectnumber = collectnumber;
    }

    public int getCommentnumber() {
        return commentnumber;
    }
    public void setCommentnumber(int commentnumber) {
        this.commentnumber = commentnumber;
    }

    public int getAgainstnumber() {
        return againstnumber;
    }
    public void setAgainstnumber(int againstnumber) {
        this.againstnumber = againstnumber;
    }

    public int getSupportnumber() {
        return supportnumber;
    }
    public void setSupportnumber(int supportnumber) {
        this.supportnumber = supportnumber;
```

```
    }
    //实现WritableComparaqble的redafields()方法,以便该数据能被序列化后完成网络传输
或文件输入。
    @Override
    public void readFields(DataInput in) throws IOException {
        daynumber = in.readInt();
        collectnumber = in.readInt();
        commentnumber = in.readInt();
        againstnumber = in.readInt();
        supportnumber = in.readInt();
    }

    //实现WritableComparaqble的write()方法,以便该数据能被反序列化后完成网络传输或文件
输入。
    @Override
    public void write(DataOutput out) throws IOException {
        out.writeInt(daynumber);
        out.writeInt(collectnumber);
        out.writeInt(commentnumber);
        out.writeInt(againstnumber);
        out.writeInt(supportnumber);
    }

    //使用compareTo对其中的数据进行比较
    @Override
    public int compareTo(Object o) {
        return 0;
    };
}
```

(2)然后新建一个class为"TvPlayInputFormat"。

自定义一个TVInputFormat类取继承FileInputFormat文件输入格式这个"父类",然后对createRecordReader()方法进行重写,其实质则是重写TVRecordReader()这个方法,得到其返回值,利用TVRecordReader()这个方法去继承RecordReader()这个方法。

```
package hadoop.tv;
import java.io.IOException;
```

```java
import org.apache.hadoop.conf.Configuration;
import org.apache.hadoop.fs.FSDataInputStream;
import org.apache.hadoop.fs.FileSystem;
import org.apache.hadoop.fs.Path;
import org.apache.hadoop.io.Text;
import org.apache.hadoop.mapreduce.InputSplit;
import org.apache.hadoop.mapreduce.RecordReader;
import org.apache.hadoop.mapreduce.TaskAttemptContext;
import org.apache.hadoop.mapreduce.lib.input.FileInputFormat;
import org.apache.hadoop.mapreduce.lib.input.FileSplit;
import org.apache.hadoop.util.LineReader;

public class TvPlayInputFormat extends FileInputFormat< Text,TvPlayWritable> {

    @Override
    public RecordReader< Text, TvPlayWritable> createRecordReader(InputSplit input,
        TaskAttemptContext context) throws IOException, InterruptedException {
        return new TVPlayRecordReader();
    }

    public class TVPlayRecordReader extends RecordReader< Text, TvPlayWritable> {

        //自定义行读取器
        public LineReader in;
        //声明 key 类型
        public Text lineKey;
        //自定义 value
        public TvPlayWritable lineValue;
        //每行数据类型
        public Text line;

        @Override
        public void close() throws IOException {
            if(in ! = null){
                in.close();
            }
        }
```

```java
//获取当前 key
@Override
public Text getCurrentKey() throws IOException, InterruptedException {
    return lineKey;
}

//获取当前 value
@Override
 public TvPlayWritable getCurrentValue() throws IOException, InterruptedException {
    return lineValue;
}

//获取当前进程
@Override
public float getProgress() throws IOException, InterruptedException {
    return 0;
}

//初始化
@Override
public void initialize(InputSplit input, TaskAttemptContext context)
        throws IOException, InterruptedException {

    FileSplit split= (FileSplit)input;   //获取分片内容
    Configuration job= context.getConfiguration();   //读取配置信息
    Path file= split.getPath();   //获取路径
    FileSystem fs= file.getFileSystem(job);   //获取文件系统

    FSDataInputStream filein= fs.open(file); //通过文件系统打开文件,对文件进行读取

    in= new LineReader(filein,job);
    line= new Text();    //新建一个 Text 实例作为自定义输入格式的 key
    lineKey= new Text();
    lineValue = new TvPlayWritable();
}

@Override
public boolean nextKeyValue() throws IOException, InterruptedException {
```

```
            // TODO Auto-generated method stub

            int linesize= in.readLine(line);
            if(linesize= = 0)
                return false;
            //读取每行数据解数组 i
            String[] pieces = line.toString().split("\t");
            if(pieces.length ! = 7){
                throw new IOException("Invalid record received");
            }
            //自定义 key 和 value 的值
            lineKey.set(pieces[0]+ "\t"+ pieces[1]);//电视剧名称和所属视频网站
            lineValue.set(Integer.parseInt(pieces[2]),Integer.parseInt(pieces[3]),
Integer.parseInt(pieces[4])
                    ,Integer.parseInt(pieces[5]),Integer.parseInt(pieces[6]));

            return true;
        }
    }
}
```

(3)写 MapReduce 统计程序,使用 MapperReducer 对输入的数据进行相应的处理,输出想要得到的结果。

在 reduce 定义一个多输出的对象 MultipleOutputs。

运行 run 函数对作业进行运行,并自定义输出 MultipleOutputs 函数调用 addNameoutput 方法对其进行设置多路径的输出。

```
package hadoop.tv;

import java.io.IOException;

import org.apache.hadoop.conf.Configuration;
import org.apache.hadoop.conf.Configured;
import org.apache.hadoop.fs.FileSystem;
import org.apache.hadoop.fs.Path;
import org.apache.hadoop.io.Text;
import org.apache.hadoop.mapreduce.Job;
```

```java
import org.apache.hadoop.mapreduce.Mapper;
import org.apache.hadoop.mapreduce.Reducer;
import org.apache.hadoop.mapreduce.lib.input.FileInputFormat;
import org.apache.hadoop.mapreduce.lib.output.FileOutputFormat;
import org.apache.hadoop.mapreduce.lib.output.MultipleOutputs;
import org.apache.hadoop.mapreduce.lib.output.TextOutputFormat;
import org.apache.hadoop.util.Tool;
import org.apache.hadoop.util.ToolRunner;

public class tvPlay extends Configured implements Tool {
    /* *
     * @ input Params Text TvPlayData
     * @ output Params Text TvPlayData
     * @ author yangjun
     * @ function 直接输出
     * /
    public static class TVPlayMapper extends
            Mapper< Text, TvPlayWritable, Text, TvPlayWritable> {
        @ Override
        protected void map(Text key, TvPlayWritable value, Context context)
                throws IOException, InterruptedException {
            context.write(key, value);
        }
    }
    /* *
     * @ input Params Text TvPlayData
     * @ output Params Text Text
     * @ author yangjun
     * @ fuction 统计每部电视剧的 点播数 收藏数等  按 source 输出到不同文件夹下
     * /
    public static class TVPlayReducer extends
            Reducer< Text, TvPlayWritable, Text, Text> {
        private Text m_key =  new Text();
        private Text m_value =  new Text();
        private MultipleOutputs< Text, Text> mos;


        protected void setup(Context context) throws IOException,
```

```
            InterruptedException {
        mos = new MultipleOutputs<Text, Text> (context);
    }//将 MultipleOutputs 的初始化放在 setup() 中,因为在 setup() 只会被调用一次
    //定义 reduce() 方法里的 multipleOutputs.write(…)。你需要把以前的 context.write
(…) 替换成现在的这个
    protected void reduce(Text Key, Iterable<TvPlayWritable> Values,
            Context context) throws IOException, InterruptedException {
        int daynumber = 0;
        int collectnumber = 0;
        int commentnumber = 0;
int againstnumber = 0;
        int supportnumber = 0;
        for (TvPlayWritable tv : Values) {
            daynumber += tv.getDaynumber();
            collectnumber += tv.getCollectnumber();
            commentnumber += tv.getCommentnumber();
            againstnumber += tv.getAgainstnumber();
            supportnumber += tv.getSupportnumber();
        }

        //tvname   source
        String[] records = Key.toString().split("\t");
        // 1 优酷 2 搜狐 3 土豆 4 爱奇艺 5 迅雷看看
        String source = records[1];//媒体类别
        m_key.set(records[0]);
        m_value.set(daynumber + "\t" + collectnumber + "\t" + commentnumber
                + "\t" + againstnumber + "\t" + supportnumber);
        if (source.equals("1")) {
            mos.write("youku", m_key, m_value);
        } else if (source.equals("2")) {
            mos.write("souhu", m_key, m_value);
        } else if (source.equals("3")) {
            mos.write("tudou", m_key, m_value);
        } else if (source.equals("4")) {
            mos.write("aiqiyi", m_key, m_value);
        } else if (source.equals("5")) {
            mos.write("xunlei", m_key, m_value);
        }
```

```java
        }

        protected void cleanup(Context context) throws IOException,
                InterruptedException {
            //关闭MultipleOutputs,也就是关闭RecordWriter,并且是一堆RecordWriter,因为
这里会有很多reduce被调用。
            mos.close();
        }
    }

    @Override
    public int run(String[] args) throws Exception {

        Configuration conf = new Configuration();//配置文件对象
        Path mypath = new Path(args[1]);
        FileSystem hdfs = mypath.getFileSystem(conf);//创建输出路径
        if (hdfs.isDirectory(mypath)) {
            hdfs.delete(mypath, true);
        }

        Job job = new Job(conf, "tvplay");//构造任务
        job.setJarByClass(tvPlay.class);//设置主类

        job.setMapperClass(TVPlayMapper.class);//设置Mapper
        job.setMapOutputKeyClass(Text.class);// key输出类型
        job.setMapOutputValueClass(TvPlayWritable.class);// value输出类型
        job.setInputFormatClass(TvPlayInputFormat.class);//自定义输入格式

        job.setReducerClass(TVPlayReducer.class);//设置Reducer
        job.setOutputKeyClass(Text.class);// reduce key类型
        job.setOutputValueClass(Text.class);// reduce value类型

        //自定义文件输出格式,通过路径名(pathname)来指定输出路径
        MultipleOutputs.addNamedOutput(job, "youku", TextOutputFormat.class,
                Text.class, Text.class);
        MultipleOutputs.addNamedOutput(job, "souhu", TextOutputFormat.class,
                Text.class, Text.class);
        MultipleOutputs.addNamedOutput(job, "tudou", TextOutputFormat.class,
```

```java
            Text.class, Text.class);
        MultipleOutputs.addNamedOutput(job, "aiqiyi", TextOutputFormat.class,
            Text.class, Text.class);
        MultipleOutputs.addNamedOutput(job, "xunlei", TextOutputFormat.class,
            Text.class, Text.class);

        FileInputFormat.addInputPath(job, new Path(args[0]));//输入路径
        FileOutputFormat.setOutputPath(job, new Path(args[1]));// 输出路径
        job.waitForCompletion(true);
        return 0;
    }


    public static void main(String[] args) throws Exception {
        String[] args0 = { "hdfs://localhost:9000/tvplay/tvplay.txt",
            "hdfs://localhost:9000/tvplay/tvplay-out/" };
        int ec = ToolRunner.run(new Configuration(), new tvPlay(), args0);
        //public static int run(Configuration conf,Tool tool, String[] args),可以在job
运行的时候指定配置文件或其他参数
        //这个方法调用 tool 的 run(String[])方法,并使用 conf 中的参数,以及 args 中的参数,而
args 一般来源于命令行。
        System.exit(ec);
    }
}
```

2)在项目中引入 hadoop 的 jar 包

(1)首先,从 https://archive.apache.org/dist/hadoop/common/hadoop-2.6.0/下载 hadoop-2.6.0.tar.gz 到客户端并解压。

(2)右键点击工程名→bulid path→最后一个选项→Libraries→Add External JARS...

(3)找到刚才解压的文件,并找到目录:/hadoop-2.6.0/share/hadoop,将下面的 common、hdfs、mapreduce、YARN 里面的全部.jar 包选中→OK,继续 Add External→common、hdfs、mapreduce、YARN 这四个文件下的 lib 的目录下的所有的 jar 包全选→OK。

3)将项目打包

(1)右键点击包"hadoop.tv"→Export..→java→JAR file→JAR file:(写入路径)\Desktop\tvplay.jar,并选中项目中的.classpath 文件和.project 文件,如下图所示:

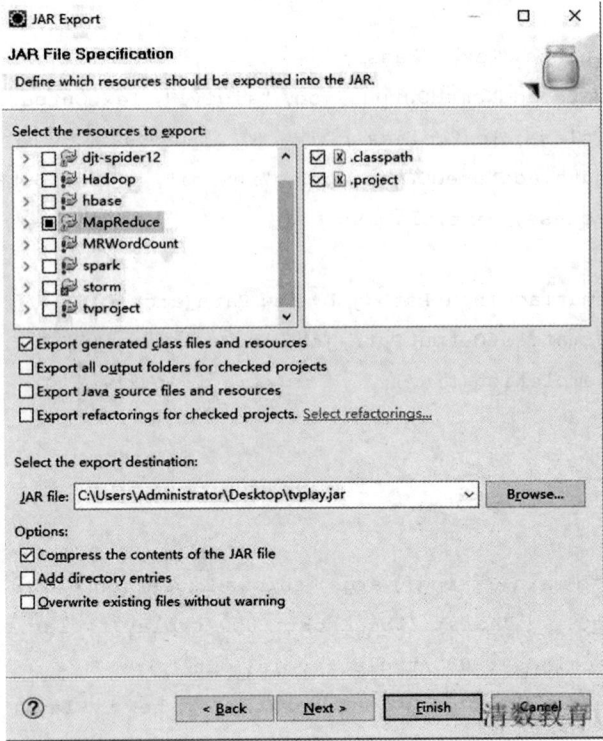

（2）点击项目"MapReduce"→"src"→"hadoop.tv"确认 TvPlayWritable、TvPlayInputFormat、tvPlay 均打入 jar 包中，如下图所示：

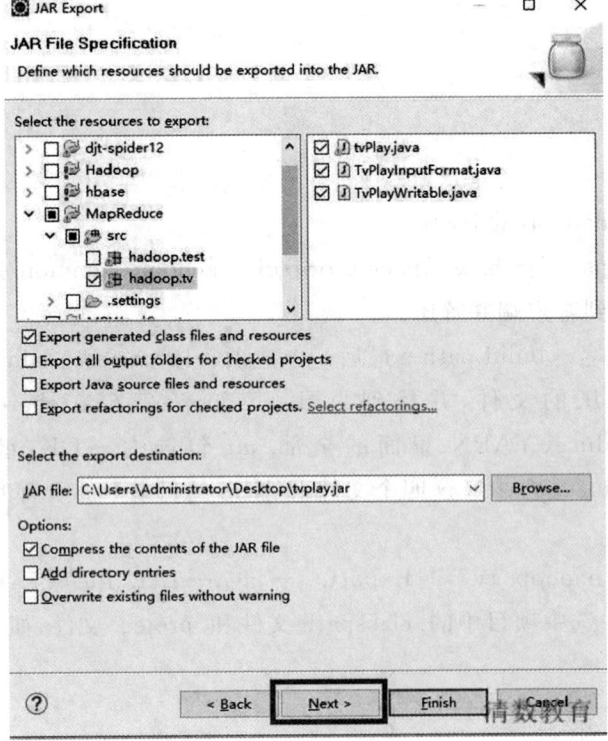

（3）选择上图中最下面一行的"next"→"next"→"Browse"，如下图所示：

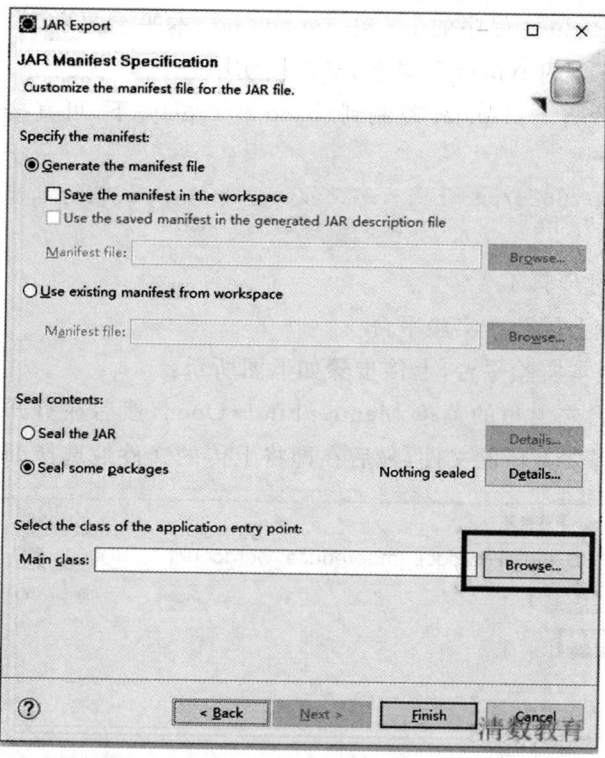

（4）在弹出来的框中，看到类"tvplay"及其位置正确后，选择"OK"：

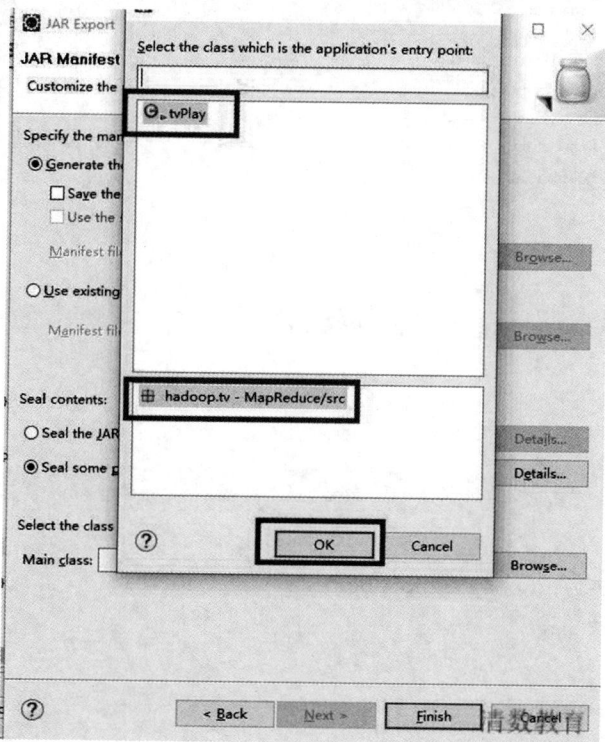

(5)选中 Finish 完成打 jar 包:

本次实验的 MapReduce 程序的 jar 包:tvplay.jar,本平台已将其放至共享目录/home/ds/data/tools/project/下的 tvplay 目录下,请直接使用。

只要使用如下命令将 tvplay.jar 复制到/hadoop/tvplay/下,可直接进行步骤 5。

```
$   cp /home/ds/data/tools/project/tvplay/tvplay.jar /hadoop/tvplay/
```

这时候就可以跳过步骤 4。

4)将项目的 jar 包上传至本实验平台

将该 jar 包上传至本实验平台,上传步骤如下图所示:

首先点击实验平台左上角的菜单 Menu→File→Open,然后在打开的新页面中选择页面右上角的 Upload,选择要上传的文件,最后在即将上传的文件处选择 Upload 即可。

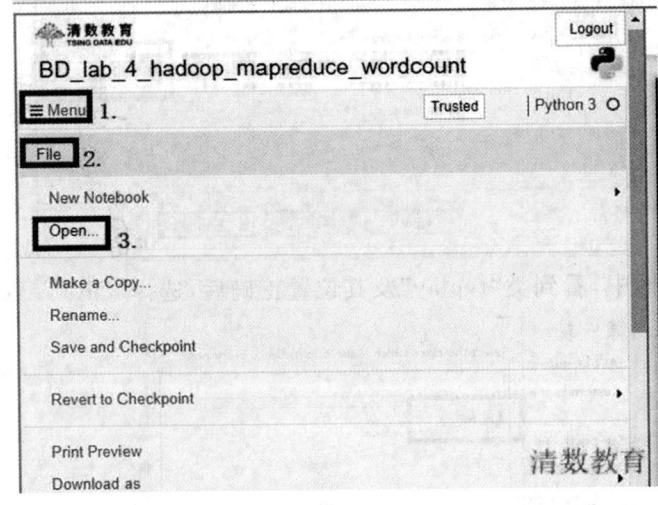

上传后的文件所在文件夹为:/home/ds/notebooks

```
$   cd /home/ds/notebooks
$   ls -l
```

将其复制到/hadoop/tvplay/目录下

```
$ cp /home/ds/notebooks/tvplay.jar /hadoop/tvplay/
$ cd /hadoop/tvplay/
$ ls -l
```

```
hadoop@2753234681ab:/home/ds/notebooks$ cp /home/ds/notebooks/Star.jar /hadoop/actor/
hadoop@2753234681ab:/home/ds/notebooks$ cd /hadoop/actor/
hadoop@2753234681ab:~/actor$ ls -l
total 12
-rw-r--r-- 1 hadoop hadoop 2154 Jun  6 03:12 actor.txt
-rw-r--r-- 1 hadoop hadoop 8121 Jun  6 03:40 Star.jar
hadoop@2753234681ab:/actor$
```

5. 运行该实例

```
$ cd /hadoop/tvplay/
$ hadoop jar /hadoop/tvplay/tvplay.jar hadoop.tv.tvplay
```

```
hadoop@5eb4c20e287d:~/tvplay$ cp /home/ds/data/tools/project/tvplay/tvplay.jar /hadoop/tvplay/
hadoop@5eb4c20e287d:~/tvplay$ hadoop jar /hadoop/tvplay/tvplay.jar hadoop.tv.tvplay
18/06/06 07:29:14 INFO client.RMProxy: Connecting to ResourceManager at /0.0.0.0:8032
18/06/06 07:29:15 WARN mapreduce.JobSubmitter: Hadoop command-line option parsing not performed.
 the Tool interface and execute your application with ToolRunner to remedy this.
18/06/06 07:29:15 INFO input.FileInputFormat: Total input paths to process : 1
18/06/06 07:29:15 INFO mapreduce.JobSubmitter: number of splits:1
18/06/06 07:29:15 INFO mapreduce.JobSubmitter: Submitting tokens for job: job_1528269819458_0001
18/06/06 07:29:15 INFO impl.YarnClientImpl: Submitted application application_1528269819458_0001
18/06/06 07:29:15 INFO mapreduce.Job: The url to track the job: http://5eb4c20e287d:8088/proxy/
_1528269819458_0001/
18/06/06 07:29:15 INFO mapreduce.Job: Running job: job_1528269819458_0001
18/06/06 07:29:21 INFO mapreduce.Job: Job job_1528269819458_0001 running in uber mode : false
18/06/06 07:29:21 INFO mapreduce.Job:  map 0% reduce 0%
18/06/06 07:29:28 INFO mapreduce.Job:  map 100% reduce 0%
18/06/06 07:29:34 INFO mapreduce.Job:  map 100% reduce 100%
18/06/06 07:29:34 INFO mapreduce.Job: Job job_1528269819458_0001 completed successfully
18/06/06 07:29:35 INFO mapreduce.Job: Counters: 49
        File System Counters
                FILE: Number of bytes read=13317883
                FILE: Number of bytes written=26853147
                FILE: Number of read operations=0
                FILE: Number of large read operations=0
                FILE: Number of write operations=0
                HDFS: Number of bytes read=10834027
                HDFS: Number of bytes written=195234
                HDFS: Number of read operations=6
                HDFS: Number of large read operations=0
                HDFS: Number of write operations=7
        Job Counters
                Launched map tasks=1
                Launched reduce tasks=1
                Data-local map tasks=1
                Total time spent by all maps in occupied slots (ms)=4144
                Total time spent by all reduces in occupied slots (ms)=3985
                Total time spent by all map tasks (ms)=4144
                Total time spent by all reduce tasks (ms)=3985
                Total vcore-seconds taken by all map tasks=4144
```

```
Total time spent by all map tasks (ms)=4144
Total time spent by all reduce tasks (ms)=3985
Total vcore-seconds taken by all map tasks=4144
Total vcore-seconds taken by all reduce tasks=3985
Total megabyte-seconds taken by all map tasks=4243456
Total megabyte-seconds taken by all reduce tasks=4080640
Map-Reduce Framework
    Map input records=332865
    Map output records=332865
    Map output bytes=12652147
    Map output materialized bytes=13317883
    Input split bytes=104
    Combine input records=0
    Combine output records=0
    Reduce input groups=5741
    Reduce shuffle bytes=13317883
    Reduce input records=332865
    Reduce output records=
    Spilled Records=665730
    Shuffled Maps =1
    Failed Shuffles=0
    Merged Map outputs=1
    GC time elapsed (ms)=81
    CPU time spent (ms)=5320
    Physical memory (bytes) snapshot=579350528
    Virtual memory (bytes) snapshot=1789083648
    Total committed heap usage (bytes)=400031744
Shuffle Errors
    BAD_ID=0
    CONNECTION=0
    IO_ERROR=0
    WRONG_LENGTH=0
    WRONG_MAP=0
    WRONG_REDUCE=0
File Input Format Counters
    Bytes Read=10833923
File Output Format Counters
    Bytes Written=0
hadoop@5eb4c20e287d:~/tvplay$
```

五、实验结果

在 hdfs 上查看结果：

```
$ hadoop fs -ls -R  /tvplay/tvplay-out/
```

通过上述命令可以看到优酷、搜狐、土豆、爱奇艺以及迅雷看看均对应了一个输出文件，如下图所示：

```
hadoop@5eb4c20e287d:~/tvplay$ hadoop fs -ls -R  /tvplay/tvplay-out/
-rw-r--r--   1 hadoop supergroup          0 2018-06-06 07:29 /tvplay/tvplay-out/_SUCCESS
-rw-r--r--   1 hadoop supergroup      38040 2018-06-06 07:29 /tvplay/tvplay-out/aiqiyi-r-00000
-rw-r--r--   1 hadoop supergroup          0 2018-06-06 07:29 /tvplay/tvplay-out/part-r-
-rw-r--r--   1 hadoop supergroup      32055 2018-06-06 07:29 /tvplay/tvplay-out/souhu-r-00000
-rw-r--r--   1 hadoop supergroup      34725 2018-06-06 07:29 /tvplay/tvplay-out/tudou-r-00000
-rw-r--r--   1 hadoop supergroup      28833 2018-06-06 07:29 /tvplay/tvplay-out/xunlei-r-00000
-rw-r--r--   1 hadoop supergroup      61581 2018-06-06 07:29 /tvplay/tvplay-out/youku-r-00000
hadoop@5eb4c20e287d:~/tvplay$
```

通过如下命令来查看搜狐的输出文件：

```
$ hadoop fs -cat /tvplay/tvplay-out/souhu-r-00000
```

大家可以使用这些命令查看其他文件的内容。

```
hadoop@5eb4c20e287d:~/tvplay$ hadoop fs -cat /tvplay/tvplay-out/souhu-r-00000
18岁             493539     0                0                     29          37
18岁29岁                     286067   0                0           20
49日             525327     0                3
AA制生活                     1750926  0                0           205         2615
BIG             1015700    0                      54         556
Good  Doctor               2394247  0                0           235         1981
Happy!Rose  Day  28233     0                7                    33
High  Kick  翘腿的反击         16708054         0              0           128          1071
I  DO  I  DO              2977995   0                      104         907
IRIS            1002029    0                2                24
IRIS2           11471709             0                76          250
May   Queen                1642308  0                0           96          561
Midas           12391021            0                0                      5
Miss欧巴桑         89153               0                14          20
Oh  My  Lady               18066713 0                0           9                    8
The    Virus               2276628  0                0           18          49
Who  Are  You              5417417  0                0           23          232
W的悲剧          41470      0                0                      3
X女特工         7935516    0                      1009       3834
sign            70714                0                0                       3
test大武生         33                  0                               0
一仆二主                     114843698          0               0           23          51
一代枭雄                      84592546          0               0           501         1355
一吻定情                      2428262           0               52          593
一场风花雪月的事                 92336    0                0           12          15
一枝梅          253672     0                36               251
一触即发                     112132847          0                          14          196
一起来看流星雨    4187080    0                0           1111       2588
一闪一闪亮晶晶    358560    0                4                     11
丈夫死                        230346   0                6                     4
丈夫的秘密                    4803247   0                36               47
丈母娘来了                    1165625   0                100              227
三十岁,你好                  5740891   0                21               48
三叶草          2070593    0                3                 42
三国霁          562040               0                297        64
```

第五章　商业大数据分析

实验7　大数据分析
——利用 hive 对预处理后的收视数据进行统计分析实验

一、实验介绍

1. 实验内容

sqoop 将数据从 hdfs 导出。

2. 数据集

这里我们使用的数据集为实验"实战项目：用 hive 分析'余额宝'躺着赚大钱背后的逻辑"的分析结果。

二、实验要求

1. Java（需要安装 1.6.x 及其以上版本）

在终端输入 java -version 来查看 Java 版本，这里我们使用的是 1.7 版本。

```
$ java -version
java version "1.7.0_121"
OpenJDK Runtime Environment (IcedTea 2.6.8) (7u121-2.6.8-1ubuntu0.14.04.3)
OpenJDK 64-Bit Server VM (build 24.121-b00, mixed mode)
```

2. hadoop 和 sqoop

在这里，我们使用了 hadoop V2.6.0 版本以及 sqoop-1.4.6 版本。

三、实验步骤

1. 实验前准备

```
$ su - hadoop
口令输入：hadoop
```

```
$ bash
$ echo $ HADOOP_HOME
/hadoop/hadoop
```

上述输出确认 hadoop 的环境变量设置有效,如果无效则激活环境变量:
```
$ source ~ /.bash_profile
```

启动 ssh,口令输入:hadoop
```
hadoop@ 357987c120a9:~ $ sudoservice ssh start
[sudo] password for hadoop:
[ ok ] Starting OpenBSD Secure Shell server: sshd.
hadoop@ 357987c120a9:~ $
```

2. 启动 hadoop

启动命令为:
```
$ start-all.sh
```

检查是否运行成功
执行 jps 命令可以查看到 hadoop 的几个主要进程:
```
$ jps

288 NameNode
528 SecondaryNameNode
367 DataNode
753 NodeManager
1063 Jps
```

3. 启动 MySQL

```
$ sudo service mysql start
```

4. 将 hive 表的数据导出到 MySQL 中

1)首先我们来看下数据集

```
$ hadoop fs -ls /user/hive/warehouse
$ hadoop fs -ls /user/hive/warehouse/stock_partition
$ hadoop fs -ls -R /user/hive/warehouse/stock_partition/tradedate= 20130726
$ hadoop fs -cat /user/hive/warehouse/stock_partition/tradedate= 20130726/000000_0
```

下图是 hive 里的数据：

这里我们以/user/hive/warehouse/stock_partition/tradedate＝20130726 为例。

2)将 hive 表的数据导入 MySQL 中

(1)先登录 MySQL,建立输出表：stock_partition_copy

第一,我们回顾下 hive 里建立的分区表 stock_partition 的结构。因为 MySQL 中建立的输出表 stock_partition_copy 结构要与该表结构相同。

```
启动 hive
$ cd /hadoop/app/hive
$ ./bin/hive


查看 stock_partition 表的结构
hive> DESC stock_partition;
```

第五章 商业大数据分析

```
hive> DESC stock_partition;
OK
tradetime               string
stockid                 string
buyprice                double
buysize                 int
sellprice               double
sellsize                int
tradedate               string

# Partition Information
# col_name              data_type           comment

tradedate               string
Time taken: 1.046 seconds, Fetched: 12 row(s)
hive>
```

由上图和下图建立表 stock_partition 的语句可知,该表有 tradetime、stockid、buyprice、buysize、sellprice、sellsize 6 个字段,tradedate 为分区 ID。

因此,MySQL 要建立的输出表 stock_partition_copy 应包含 radetime、stockid、buyprice、buysize、sellprice、sellsize 6 个字段。

```
hive> create table if not exists stock_partition (tradetime STRING,stockid STRING,buyprice DOUBLE,
INT,sellprice DOUBLE,sellsize INT)
     > partitioned by (tradedate STRING) row format delimited fields terminated by ',';
OK
Time taken: 0.054 seconds
hive>
```

第二,登录 MySQL,用户名为 hive,密码为 hive。

```
$ mysql -h localhost -u hive -p
Enter password:输入 root 回车即可


mysql> use hive;
Reading table information for completion of table and column names
You can turn off this feature to get a quicker startup with -A

Database changed

mysql> create table stock_partition_copy (tradetime text, stockid text, buyprice
double,buysize int,sellprice
double,sellsize int);
Query OK, 0 rows affected (0.01 sec)
```

第三,退出 MySQL。

```
mysql> exit
```

(2)使用 sqoop 将 hive 分析的结果导入 MySQL 数据库。

```
$ sqoop export --connect jdbc:mysql://127.0.0.1/hive  --username root --password root --table stock_partition_copy --export-dir /user/hive/warehouse/stock_partition/tradedate=20130726 --input-fields-terminated-by ","
```

四、实验结果

登录 MySQL,用户名为 hive,密码为 hive。

```
$ mysql -h localhost -u hive -p
Enter password:输入 root 回车即可
```

```
mysql> use hive;

mysql> select * from stock_partition_copy;
```

退出 MySQL

```
mysql> exit
```

数据库中查看结果如下图所示：

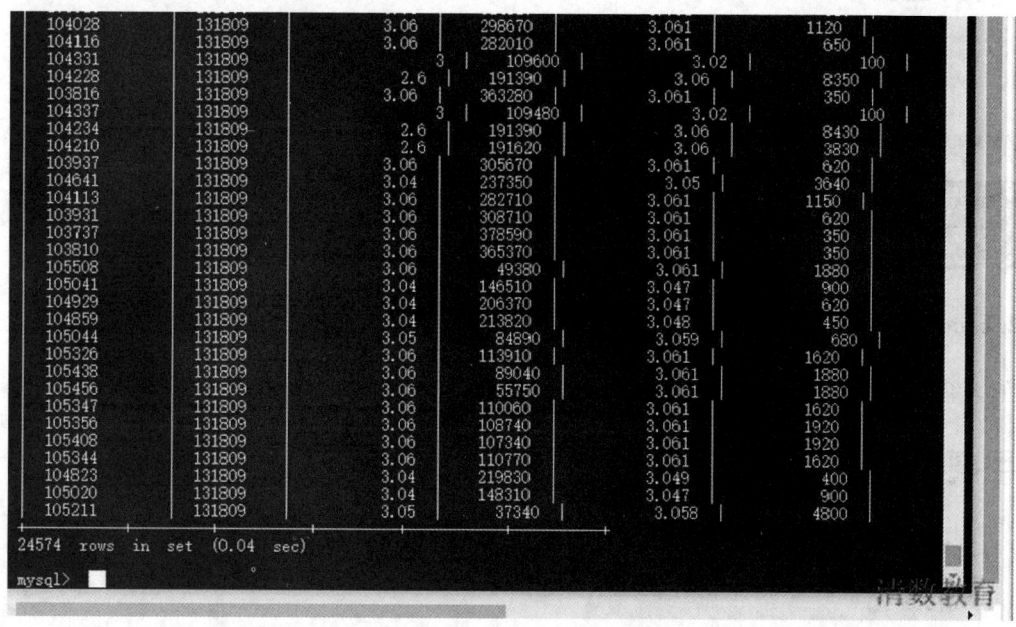

五、练习题

请以 /user/hive/warehouse/stock_partition/tradedate＝20130722 为例，利用 sqoop 将数据导入 MySQL 数据库。

将你执行的命令和输出的结果粘贴到下面的文本框中。

作业练习：

＃＃＃输入你的作业代码＃＃＃

＃＃＃作业代码结束＃＃＃

实验 8　sqoop 安装部署及数据结果利用 hdfs 导入实验

一、实验介绍

实验内容：sqoop 将数据导入到 hdfs。

二、实验要求

1. Java（需要安装 1.6.x 及其以上版本）

在终端输入 java -version 来查看 Java 版本，这里我们使用的是 1.7 版本。

```
$ java -version
java version "1.7.0_121"
OpenJDK Runtime Environment (IcedTea 2.6.8) (7u121-2.6.8-1ubuntu0.14.04.3)
OpenJDK 64-Bit Server VM (build 24.121-b00, mixed mode)
```

2. hadoop 和 sqoop

在这里，我们使用了 hadoop V2.6.0 版本以及 sqoop-1.4.6 版本。

三、实验步骤

（一）实验前准备

```
$ su - hadoop
口令输入：hadoop


$ bash
$ echo $HADOOP_HOME
/hadoop/hadoop
```

上述输出确认 hadoop 的环境变量设置有效，如果无效则激活环境变量：

```
$ source ~/.bash_profile
```

启动 ssh，口令输入：hadoop

```
hadoop@357987c120a9:~ $ sudo service ssh start
[sudo] password for hadoop:
```

```
[ ok ] Starting OpenBSD Secure Shell server: sshd.
hadoop@ 357987c120a9:~ $
```

(二)启动 hadoop

```
启动命令为:
$ start-all.sh
检查是否运行成功
# 执行 jps 命令可以查看到 hadoop 的几个主要进程:
$ jps
288 NameNode
528 SecondaryNameNode
367 DataNode
753 NodeManager
1063 Jps
```

(三)启动 MySQL

```
$ sudo service mysql start
```

(四)sqoop 将数据导入 hdfs——sqoop Import hdfs

1. sqoop Import 应用场景——密码访问

1)明码访问

登录 MySQL,用户名为 root,密码为 root。

```
$ mysql -u root -p
Enter password:输入 root 回车即可
```

查看 MySQL 中的数据库。

```
mysql> show databases;
+--------------------+
| Database           |
+--------------------+
```

```
| information_schema  |
| hive                |
| mysql               |
| performance_schema  |
| sys                 |
+---------------------+
5 rows in set (0.00 sec)
mysql>
```

退出 MySQL。

```
mysql> exit
```

```
$ sqoop list-databases --connect jdbc:mysql://127.0.0.1 --username root --password root
```

说明：

sqoop list-databases 列出数据库。

--connect jdbc:mysql://127.0.0.1 连接 MySQL 数据库。

--username root 为 MySQL 数据库的用户。

--password root 为 MySQL 数据库的密码。

执行以上命令后连接数据库并将 MySQL 中的数据库打印出来，如下图所示：

2）交互式密码

```
$ sqoop list-databases --connect jdbc:mysql://127.0.0.1 --username root -P
```
当出现"Enter password:"时，输入密码为 root，回车即可

第五章　商业大数据分析

```
hadoop@03a77e5063cc:/home/ds/data/tools$ sqoop list-databases --connect jdbc:mysql://127.0.0.1 --username root -P
Warning: /hadoop/app/sqoop/../hbase does not exist! HBase imports will fail.
Please set $HBASE_HOME to the root of your HBase installation.
Warning: /hadoop/app/sqoop/../hcatalog does not exist! HCatalog jobs will fail.
Please set $HCAT_HOME to the root of your HCatalog installation.
Warning: /hadoop/app/sqoop/../accumulo does not exist! Accumulo imports will fail.
Please set $ACCUMULO_HOME to the root of your Accumulo installation.
Warning: /hadoop/app/sqoop/../zookeeper does not exist! Accumulo imports will fail.
Please set $ZOOKEEPER_HOME to the root of your Zookeeper installation.
18/06/25 02:15:20 INFO sqoop.Sqoop: Running Sqoop version: 1.4.6
Enter password:
18/06/25 02:15:22 INFO manager.MySQLManager: Preparing to use a MySQL streaming resultset.
information_schema
mysql
performance_schema
sys
hadoop@03a77e5063cc:/home/ds/data/tools$
```

3）文件授权密码

（1）首先创建/hadoop/.password 文件，将 MySQL 的 root 用户的密码写进去。

```
$ cd /hadoop
$ echo -n "root" > .password
```

（2）将文件上传至 hdfs。

```
$ hadoop fs -mkdir /user
$ hadoop fs -mkdir /user/hadoop
$ hadoop fs -put /hadoop/.password /user/hadoop
```

（3）给.password 文件赋予 400 的权限。

```
$ hadoop fs -chmod 400 /user/hadoop/.password
```

（4）运行 sqoop 的命令。

```
$ sqoop list-databases --connect jdbc:mysql://127.0.0.1 --username root --password-file /user/hadoop/.password
```

2. sqoop Import 应用场景——导入全表

1）不指定目录

首先登录 MySQL 创建 test 数据库和数据库表 user。

登录 MySQL，用户名为 root，密码为 root。

```
$ mysql -u root -p
Enter password:输入 root 回车即可
```

创建 test 数据库。

```
mysql> create database test;
Query OK, 1 row affected (0.01 sec)
```

查看数据库 test 是否创建成功。

```
mysql> show databases;
+--------------------+
| Database           |
+--------------------+
| information_schema |
| mysql              |
| performance_schema |
| sys                |
| test               |
+--------------------+
5 rows in set (0.00 sec)
```

使用 test 数据库。

```
mysql> use test;
Database changed
```

创建 user 数据库表。

```
mysql> create table user(uid int auto_increment primary key,name varchar(20) not null,age int(5));
Query OK, 0 rows affected (0.01 sec)
```

插入三条数据。

```
mysql> insert into user(uid,name,age) values (1,'zhangsan',22),(2,'lisi',23),(3,'wangwu',20);
Query OK, 3 rows affected (0.00 sec)
Records: 3  Duplicates: 0  Warnings: 0
```

查看 user 表中的数据。

```
mysql> select * from user;
+-----+----------+------+
| uid | name     | age  |
+-----+----------+------+
|   1 | zhangsan |   22 |
|   2 | lisi     |   23 |
|   3 | wangwu   |   20 |
+-----+----------+------+
3 rows in set (0.00 sec)
```

退出 MySQL。

```
mysql> exit
```

因为在不指定导入目录时，sqoop 会将导入文件放入 /user/hadoop/user 目录下，所以首先查看 hdfs 的 /user/hadoop 目录。

```
$ hadoop fs -ls /user/hadoop
```

```
Bye
hadoop@ffaae710971a:~$ hadoop fs -ls /user/hadoop
Found 1 items
-r--------   1 hadoop supergroup          4 2018-06-25 09:32 /user/hadoop/.password
hadoop@ffaae710971a:~$
```

不指定目录，将数据库导入 hdfs 中：

```
$ sqoop import --connect jdbc:mysql://127.0.0.1/test --username root --password-file /user/hadoop/.password --table user
```

说明：sqoop import 使用 sqoop 导入数据。

如上图所示,在执行 MapReduce 作业时提交了 3 个 MapReduce 作业,在 MapReduce 结束时也保存了 3 条记录,所以导入 hdfs 时,在/user/hadoop/user 文件夹下,对应了 part-m-00000、part-m-00001、part-m-00002,3 个文件,实验时每个人保存的记录个数都有可能不同,但是使用 hadoop fs -cat /user/hadoop/user/part-m-* 查看,导入的结果是一样的。

再次查看 hdfs 的/user 目录。

```
$ hadoop fs -ls /user/hadoop
$ hadoop fs -ls -R /user/hadoop/user
```

查看导入的文件内容。

```
$ hadoop fs -cat /user/hadoop/user/part-m-*
```

说明:"part-m-*"中的星号"*"表示以"part-m-"开头的所有文件。

2)指定目录

指定目录,将数据库导入到 hdfs 中。

```
$ sqoop import --connect jdbc:mysql://127.0.0.1/test --username root --password-file /user/hadoop/.password --table user --target-dir /sqoop/test/user
```

说明：--target-dir /sqoop/test/user 指定导入的目录。

查看 hdfs 的 /sqoop/test/user 目录
```
$ hadoop fs -ls  -R /sqoop/test/user
```

查看导入文件的内容。

```
$ hadoop fs -cat /sqoop/test/user/part-m-*
```

3）目录已存在

```
$ sqoop import --connect jdbc:mysql://127.0.0.1/test --username root --password-file /user/hadoop/.password --table user --target-dir /sqoop/test/user --delete-target-dir
```

说明：--delete-target-dir 如果导入目录存在，先删除该目录。
查看导入文件的内容。

```
$ hadoop fs -cat /sqoop/test/user/part-m-*
```

3. sqoop Import 应用场景——控制并行度

1）控制并行度

```
$ sqoop import --connect jdbc:mysql://127.0.0.1/test --username root --password-file /user/hadoop/.password --table user --target-dir /sqoop/test/user --delete-target-dir -m 1
```

说明：-m 1 使用一个 mapreduce 来执行。

查看 hdfs 的 /sqoop/test/user 目录
```
$ hadoop fs -ls  -R /sqoop/test/user
```

因为这里只使用了一个 MapReduce 来执行，因此 hdfs 的 /user/hadoop/user 文件夹下，对应了 part-m-00000 一个文件，如下图所示：

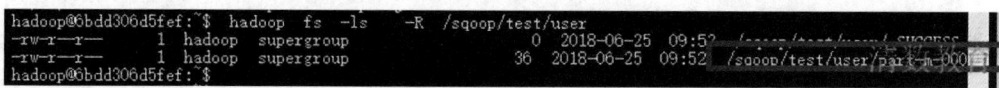

2）查看导入文件的内容。

```
$ hadoop fs -cat /sqoop/test/user/part-m-*
```

```
hadoop@6bdd306d5fef:~$ hadoop fs -cat /sqoop/test/user/part-m-*
1,zhangsan,22
2,lisi,23
3,wangwu,20
hadoop@6bdd306d5fef:~$
```

4. sqoop Import 应用场景——控制字段分隔符

1)控制字段分隔符(默认分隔符为逗号)

```
$ sqoop import --connect jdbc:mysql://127.0.0.1/test --username root --password-file /user/hadoop/.password --table user --target-dir /sqoop/test/user --delete-target-dir -m 1 --fields-terminated-by "@ "
```

2)查看导入文件的内容

```
$ hadoop fs -cat /sqoop/test/user/part-m-*
```

```
18/06/25 10:02:09 INFO mapreduce.ImportJobBase: Retrieved 3 records.
hadoop@6bdd306d5fef:~$ hadoop fs -cat /sqoop/test/user/part-m-*
1@zhangsan@22
2@lisi@23
3@wangwu@20
hadoop@6bdd306d5fef:~$
```

5. sqoop Import 应用场景——增量导入

1)手动增量导入

首先登录 MySQL。

登录 MySQL,用户名为 root,密码为 root。

```
$ mysql -u root -p
Enter password:输入 root 回车即可
```

使用 test 数据库。

```
mysql> use test;
Database changed
```

插入两条新的数据。

```
mysql>    insert into user(uid,name,age) values (4,'zhang1',24),(5,'zahng2',22);
```

查看 user 表是否新增了两条数据。

```
mysql> select * from user;
```

退出 MySQL。

```
mysql> exit
```

```
$ sqoop import --connect jdbc:mysql://127.0.0.1/test --username root --password-file /user/hadoop/.password --table user --target-dir /sqoop/test/user -m 1 --fields-terminated-by "@" --append --check-column 'uid' --incremental append --last-value 3
```

说明：
--append 增加数据到一个已经存在的 hdfs 上的数据集目录下。
--check-column 'uid' 根据"uid"字段进行增量。
--incremental append 通过"append"进行增量导入。
--last-value 3 上次导入的最大值。

查看导入文件的内容。

```
$ hadoop fs -cat /sqoop/test/user/part-m-*
```

2）自动增量导入

使用 sqoop job 进行自动增量导入。

```
$ sqoop job --create job_import_test_user -- import  --connect jdbc:mysql://127.0.0.1/
test --username root --password-file /user/hadoop/.password --table user --target-dir /
sqoop/test/user  -m 1 --fields-terminated-by "@ " --append --check-column 'uid' --
incremental append --last-value 5
```

说明：

--create job_import_test_user 创建一个叫"job_import_test_user"的 job，参数--last-value 5 会保存进来，下次再运行 job 就可以。

登录 MySQL，用户名为 root，密码为 root。

```
$ mysql -u root -p
Enter password:输入 root 回车即可
```

使用 test 数据库。

```
mysql> use test;
Database changed
```

插入两条新的数据。

```
mysql>   insert into user(uid,name) values (6,'zhaosi'),(7,'zhouwang');
```

查看 user 表是否新增了两条数据。

```
mysql>   select* from user;
```

退出 MySQL。

```
mysql>   exit
```

查看导入文件的内容。

```
$ hadoop fs -cat /sqoop/test/user/part-m-*
```

```
hadoop@112232d18b9d:~$ hadoop fs -cat /sqoop/test/user/part-m-*
1@zhangsan@22
2@lisi@23
3@wangwu@20
4@zhang1@24
5@zahng2@22
hadoop@112232d18b9d:~$
```

列举已经保存的 job。

```
$ sqoop job --list
```

```
hadoop@623330689a9f:~$    sqoop job --list
Warning: /hadoop/app/sqoop/../hbase does not exist! HBase imports will fail.
Please set $HBASE_HOME to the root of your HBase installation.
Warning: /hadoop/app/sqoop/../hcatalog does not exist! HCatalog jobs will fail.
Please set $HCAT_HOME to the root of your HCatalog installation.
Warning: /hadoop/app/sqoop/../accumulo does not exist! Accumulo imports will fail.
Please set $ACCUMULO_HOME to the root of your Accumulo installation.
Warning: /hadoop/app/sqoop/../zookeeper does not exist! Accumulo imports will fail.
Please set $ZOOKEEPER_HOME to the root of your Zookeeper installation.
18/06/25 10:29:15 INFO sqoop.Sqoop: Running Sqoop version: 1.4.6
Available jobs:
    job_import_test_user
hadoop@623330689a9f:~$
```

执行已经保存的 job。

```
$ sqoop job --exec job_import_test_user
```

```
            CPU time spent (ms)=710
            Physical memory (bytes) snapshot=229089280
            Virtual memory (bytes) snapshot=888135680
            Total committed heap usage (bytes)=201326592
    File Input Format Counters
            Bytes Read=0
    File Output Format Counters
            Bytes Written=30
18/06/25 10:25:55 INFO mapreduce.ImportJobBase: Transferred 30 bytes in 11.6594 seconds (2.573
18/06/25 10:25:55 INFO mapreduce.ImportJobBase: Retrieved 2 records.
18/06/25 10:25:55 INFO util.AppendUtils: Appending to directory user
18/06/25 10:25:55 INFO util.AppendUtils: Using found partition 2
18/06/25 10:25:55 INFO tool.ImportTool: Saving incremental import state to the metastore
18/06/25 10:25:55 INFO tool.ImportTool: Updated data for job: job_import_test_user
hadoop@623330689a9f:~$
```

查看导入文件的内容。

```
$ hadoop fs -cat /sqoop/test/user/part-m-*
```

```
job_import_test_user
hadoop@623330689a9f:~$ hadoop fs -cat /sqoop/test/user/part-m-*
1@zhangsan@22
2@lisi@23
3@wangwu@20
4@zhang1@24
5@zahng2@22
6@zhaosi@null
7@zhouwang@null
hadoop@623330689a9f:~$
```

6. sqoop Import 应用场景——启动压缩

启动压缩

```
$ sqoop import --connect jdbc:mysql://127.0.0.1/test --username root --password-file /user/hadoop/.password --table user --target-dir /sqoop/test/user --delete-target-dir -m 1 --fields-terminated-by "@ " -z
```

说明：-z 表示压缩，默认为 gzip 格式的压缩文件，即扩展名为.gz。

```
$ hadoop fs -ls -R /sqoop/test/user
```

7. sqoop Import 应用场景——导入空值处理

导入空值处理

```
$ sqoop import --connect jdbc:mysql://127.0.0.1/test --username root --password-file /user/hadoop/.password --table user --target-dir /sqoop/test/user --delete-target-dir -m 1 --fields-terminated-by "@ " --null-non-string "# # # " --null-string "# # # "
```

说明：

--null-non-string ＜null-string＞如果指定列为非字符串类型，使用指定字符串替换值为 null。

--null-string ＜null-string＞如果指定列为字符串类型，使用指定字符串替换值为 null 的该类列的值。

查看导入文件的内容。

```
$ hadoop fs -cat /sqoop/test/user/part-m-*
```

```
18/06/23 10:58:11 INFO mapreduce.ImportJobBase: Retrieved 7 record
hadoop@623330689a9f:~$ hadoop fs -cat /sqoop/test/user/part-m-*
1@zhangsan@22
2@lisi@23
3@wangwu@20
4@zhang1@24
5@zahng2@22
6@zhaosi@###
7@zhouwang@###
hadoop@623330689a9f:~$
```

8. sqoop Import 应用场景——导入部分数据

1)使用--columns

```
$ sqoop import --connect jdbc:mysql://127.0.0.1/test --username root --password-file /
user/hadoop/.password --table user --columns uid,name --target-dir /sqoop/test/user --
delete-target-dir -m 1 --fields-terminated-by "@ " --null-non-string "# # # " --null-string
"# # # "
```

说明:--columns ＜col,col,col…＞ 从表中导出指定的一组列的数据。

查看导入文件的内容。

```
$ hadoop fs -cat /sqoop/test/user/part-m-*
```

```
hadoop@623330689a9f:~$ hadoop fs -cat /sqoop/test/user/part-m-*
1@zhangsan
2@lisi
3@wangwu
4@zhang1
5@zahng2
6@zhaosi
7@zhouwang
hadoop@623330689a9f:~$
```

2)使用--where

```
$ sqoop import --connect jdbc:mysql://127.0.0.1/test --username root --password-file /
user/hadoop/.password --table user --where "age= 22" --target-dir /sqoop/test/user --
delete-target-dir -m 1 --fields-terminated-by "@ " --null-non-string "# # # " --null-string
"# # # "
```

查看导入文件的内容。

```
$ hadoop fs -cat /sqoop/test/user/part-m-*
```

3) 使用--query

如果导入比较复杂是用 query 筛选更合适。

```
$ sqoop import --connect jdbc:mysql://127.0.0.1/test --username root --password-file /user/hadoop/.password --query "select * from user where age< = 23 and \$ CONDITIONS" --target-dir /sqoop/test/user --delete-target-dir -m 1 --fields-terminated-by "@ " --null-non-string "# # # " --null-string "# # # "
```

说明：

query 中 where 后必须有 $ CONDITIONS。如果 query 后面的有引号，$ CONDITIONS 前必须有反斜杠。

查看导入文件的内容。

```
$ hadoop fs -cat /sqoop/test/user/part-m-*
```

实验 9 sqoop 安装部署及数据结果利用 hdfs 导出实验

一、实验介绍

实验内容：sqoop 将数据从 hdfs 导出。

二、实验要求

1. Java(需要安装 1.6.x 及其以上版本)

在终端输入 java -version 来查看 Java 版本，这里我们使用的是 1.7 版本。

```
$ java -version
java version "1.7.0_121"
OpenJDK Runtime Environment (IcedTea 2.6.8) (7u121-2.6.8-1ubuntu0.14.04.3)
OpenJDK 64-Bit Server VM (build 24.121-b00, mixed mode)
```

2. hadoop 和 sqoop

在这里，我们使用了 hadoop V2.6.0 版本以及 sqoop-1.4.6 版本。

三、实验步骤

1. 实验前准备

```
$ su - hadoop
口令输入:hadoop


$ bash
$ echo $ HADOOP_HOME
/hadoop/hadoop
```

上述输出确认 hadoop 的环境变量设置有效，如果无效则激活环境变量。

```
$ source ~/.bash_profile
启动 ssh,口令输入:hadoop
hadoop@ 357987c120a9:~ $ sudo service ssh start
[sudo] password for hadoop:
[ ok ] Starting OpenBSD Secure Shell server: sshd.
hadoop@ 357987c120a9:~ $
```

2. 启动 hadoop

启动命令如下。

```
$ start-all.sh
```

检查是否运行成功。

```
# 执行 jps 命令可以查看到 hadoop 的几个主要进程:
$ jps

288 NameNode
528 SecondaryNameNode
367 DataNode
753 NodeManager
1063 Jps
```

3. 启动 MySQL

```
$ sudo service mysql start
```

4. 使用文件授权密码进行访问

(1)首先创建/hadoop/.password 文件,将 MySQL 的 root 用户的密码写进去。

```
$ cd /hadoop
$ echo -n "root" > .password
```

(2)将文件上传至 hdfs。

```
$ hadoop fs -mkdir /user
$ hadoop fs -mkdir /user/hadoop
$ hadoop fs -put /hadoop/.password /user/hadoop
```

(3)给.password 文件赋予 400 的权限。

```
$ hadoop fs -chmod 400 /user/hadoop/.password
```

(4) 运行 sqoop 的命令。

```
$ sqoop list-databases --connect jdbc:mysql://127.0.0.1 --username root --password-file /user/hadoop/.password
```

5. sqoop 将数据从 hdfs 导出——sqoop Export hdfs

1) sqoop Export 应用场景——直接导出

(1) 建立数据库 export_test,再建立两个与上节课程里 user 表结构一样的表,这里分别命名为 user、user_copy。

登录 MySQL,用户名为 root,密码为 root。

```
$ mysql -u root -p
Enter password:输入 root 回车即可
```

创建 export_test 数据库。

```
mysql> create database export_test;
Query OK, 1 row affected (0.01 sec)
```

查看数据库 export_test 是创建成功。

```
mysql> show databases;
+--------------------+
| Database           |
+--------------------+
| information_schema |
| export_test        |
| hive               |
| mysql              |
| performance_schema |
| sys                |
+--------------------+
6 rows in set (0.00 sec)
```

使用 export_test 数据库。

```
mysql> use export_test;
Database changed
```

创建 user 数据库表。

```
mysql> create table user(uid int auto_increment primary key,name varchar(20) not null,age int(5));
Query OK, 0 rows affected (0.01 sec)
```

插入 3 条数据。

```
mysql> insert into user(uid,name,age) values (1,'zhangsan',22),(2,'lisi',23),(3,'wangwu',20);
Query OK, 3 rows affected (0.00 sec)
Records: 3  Duplicates: 0  Warnings: 0
```

查看 user 表中的数据。

```
mysql> select * from user;
+-----+----------+------+
| uid | name     | age  |
+-----+----------+------+
|   1 | zhangsan |   22 |
|   2 | lisi     |   23 |
|   3 | wangwu   |   20 |
+-----+----------+------+
3 rows in set (0.00 sec)
```

创建 user_copy 数据库表。

```
mysql> create table user_copy(uid int auto_increment primary key,name varchar(20) not null,age int(5));
Query OK, 0 rows affected (0.01 sec)
```

查看 user_copy 表中的数据。

```
mysql> select * from user_copy;
Empty set (0.00 sec)
```

退出 MySQL。

```
mysql> exit
```

第五章 商业大数据分析

（2）将 user 表中的数据导入到 hdfs。

我们将 user 表中的内容导入到 hdfs 的 /sqoop/export/test/user_copy 目录下。

```
$ sqoop import --connect jdbc:mysql://127.0.0.1/export_test --username root --password-file /user/hadoop/.password --table user --target-dir /sqoop/export/test/user_copy --delete-target-dir -m 1 --fields-terminated-by "@"
```

```
$ hadoop fs -cat /sqoop/export/test/user_copy/part-m-*
```

```
hadoop@7b1723229953:~$ hadoop fs -cat /sqoop/export/test/user_copy/part-m-*
1@zhangsan@22
2@lisi@23
3@wangwu@20
hadoop@7b1723229953:~$
```

（3）将刚刚导入到 hdfs 的数据，从 hdfs 导出到 MySQL。

```
$ sqoop export --connect jdbc:mysql://127.0.0.1/export_test --username root --password-file /user/hadoop/.password --table user_copy --export-dir /sqoop/export/test/user_copy --input-fields-terminated-by "@"
```

说明：

--export-dir /sqoop/export/test/user_copy 导出过程中 hdfs 源路径。

--fields-terminated-by "@" 表示字段分隔符为 "@"。

```
hadoop@7b1723229953:~$ sqoop export --connect jdbc:mysql://127.0.0.1/export_test --username root
rd-file /user/hadoop/.password --table user_copy --export-dir /sqoop/export/test/user_copy --input-
terminated-by "@"
Warning: /hadoop/app/sqoop/../hbase does not exist! HBase imports will fail.
Please set $HBASE_HOME to the root of your HBase installation.
Warning: /hadoop/app/sqoop/../hcatalog does not exist! HCatalog jobs will fail.
Please set $HCAT_HOME to the root of your HCatalog installation.
Warning: /hadoop/app/sqoop/../accumulo does not exist! Accumulo imports will fail.
Please set $ACCUMULO_HOME to the root of your Accumulo installation.
Warning: /hadoop/app/sqoop/../zookeeper does not exist! Accumulo imports will fail.
Please set $ZOOKEEPER_HOME to the root of your Zookeeper installation.
18/06/26 06:31:36 INFO sqoop.Sqoop: Running Sqoop version: 1.4.6
18/06/26 06:31:37 INFO manager.MySQLManager: Preparing to use a MySQL streaming resultset.
18/06/26 06:31:37 INFO tool.CodeGenTool: Beginning code generation
18/06/26 06:31:38 INFO manager.SqlManager: Executing SQL statement: SELECT t.* FROM user_copy AS
1
18/06/26 06:31:38 INFO manager.SqlManager: Executing SQL statement: SELECT t.* FROM user_copy AS
1
18/06/26 06:31:38 INFO orm.CompilationManager: HADOOP_MAPRED_HOME is /hadoop/hadoop
Note: /tmp/sqoop-hadoop/compile/f809cb09014ffcad784966a4ad277168/user_copy.java uses or overrides a dep
ated API.
Note: Recompile with -Xlint:deprecation for details.
18/06/26 06:31:39 INFO orm.CompilationManager: Writing jar file: /tmp/sqoop-hadoop/compile/f809cb0 14
d784966a4ad277168/user_copy.jar
18/06/26 06:31:39 INFO mapreduce.ExportJobBase: Beginning export of user_copy
18/06/26 06:31:39 INFO Configuration.deprecation: mapred.jar is deprecated. Instead, use mapreduce.j
18/06/26 06:31:39 INFO Configuration.deprecation: mapred.reduce.tasks.speculative.execution is deprec
  Instead, use mapreduce.reduce.speculative
18/06/26 06:31:39 INFO Configuration.deprecation: mapred.map.tasks.speculative.execution is deprec
stead, use mapreduce.map.speculative
```

(4) 导出后登录 MySQL 查看 user_copy 表中内容。

登录 MySQL，用户名为 root，密码为 root。

```
$ mysql -u root -p
Enter password:输入 root 回车即可
```

```
mysql> use export_test;
Reading table information for completion of table and column names
You can turn off this feature to get a quicker startup with -A
```

查看 user-copy 表中的数据。

```
mysql>    select * from user_copy;
```

退出 MySQL。

```
mysql> exit
```

2) sqoop Export 应用场景——指定 map 数

(1)登录 MySQL,删除数据库表 user_copy 中的内容。

登录 MySQL,用户名为 root,密码为 root。

```
$ mysql -u root -p
Enter password:输入 root 回车即可
```

使用 export_test 数据库。

```
mysql> use export_test;
Reading table information for completion of table and column names
You can turn off this feature to get a quicker startup with -A

mysql> select * from user_copy;
+-----+----------+------+
| uid | name     | age  |
+-----+----------+------+
|   1 | zhangsan |   22 |
|   2 | lisi     |   23 |
|   3 | wangwu   |   20 |
+-----+----------+------+
3 rows in set (0.00 sec)
```

```
mysql> delete from user_copy;
Query OK, 2 rows affected (0.00 sec)
```

```
mysql> select * from user_copy;
Empty set (0.00 sec)
```

退出 MySQL。

```
mysql> exit
```

(2)指定 map 数将数据从 hdfs 导出。

```
$ sqoop export - connect jdbc:mysql://127.0.0.1/export_test - username root - password-file /user/adoop/.password - table user_copy - export-dir /sqoop/export/test/user_copy - input-fields-terminated-by "@" -m 1
```

(3)导出后登录 MySQL 查看 user_copy 表中内容。

登录 MySQL,用户名为 root,密码为 root。

```
$ mysql -u root -p
Enter password:输入 root 回车即可
```

```
mysql> use export_test;
Database changed
```

查看 user_copy 表中的数据。

```
mysql> select * from user_copy;
```

退出 MySQL。

```
mysql> exit
```

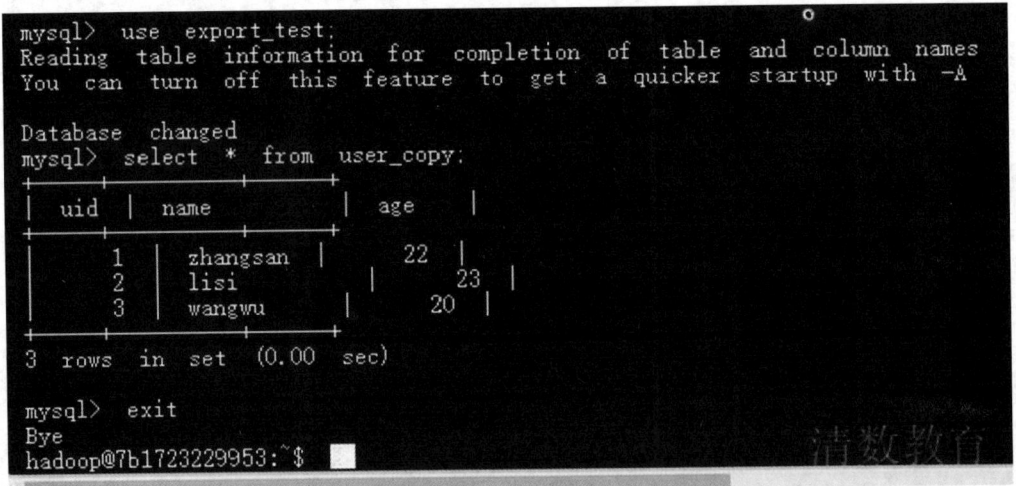

3)sqoop Export 应用场景——插入和更新

(1)手动增量导入到 hdfs。

首先登录 MySQL。

登录 MySQL,用户名为 root,密码为 root。

```
$ mysql -u root -p
Enter password:输入 root 回车即可
```

使用 export_test 数据库。

```
mysql>  use export_test;
Reading table information for completion of table and column names
You can turn off this feature to get a quicker startup with -A

Database changed
```

插入两条新的数据。

```
mysql>  insert into user(uid,name,age) values (4,'zhang1',24),(5,'zahng2',22);
Query OK, 2 rows affected (0.01 sec)
Records: 2  Duplicates: 0  Warnings: 0
```

查看 user 表是否新增了两条数据。

```
mysql>  select * from user;
+-----+----------+------+
| uid | name     | age  |
+-----+----------+------+
|   1 | zhangsan |   22 |
|   2 | lisi     |   23 |
|   3 | wangwu   |   20 |
|   4 | zhang1   |   24 |
|   5 | zahng2   |   22 |
+-----+----------+------+
5 rows in set (0.00 sec)
```

修改 user_copy 一些字段的值,来观察待会是否会更新数据。

```
mysql>  update user_copy set age= 100 where age< = 100;
Query OK, 3 rows affected (0.01 sec)
Rows matched: 3  Changed: 3  Warnings: 0
```

查看是否修改了 user_copy 表中的数据。

```
mysql>  select * from user_copy;
+-----+----------+------+
| uid | name     | age  |
```

```
+-----+----------+------+
|  1  | zhangsan | 100  |
|  2  | lisi     | 100  |
|  3  | wangwu   | 100  |
+-----+----------+------+
3 rows in set (0.00 sec)
```

退出 MySQL。

```
mysql> exit
```

增量导入。

```
$ sqoop import --connect jdbc:mysql://127.0.0.1/export_test --username root --password-file /user/hadoop/.password --table user --target-dir /sqoop/export/test/user_copy -m 1 --fields-terminated-by "@" --append --check-column 'uid' --incremental append --last-value 3
```

查看导入文件的内容。

```
$ hadoop fs -cat /sqoop/export/test/user_copy/part-m-*
```

```
                    Bytes Read=0
         File Output Format Counters
                   Bytes Written=24
18/06/26  06:39:15 INFO mapreduce.ImportJobBase: Transferred 24 bytes in 13.4382 seconds (1.786 byt
18/06/26  06:39:15 INFO mapreduce.ImportJobBase: Retrieved 2 records.
18/06/26  06:39:15 INFO util.AppendUtils: Appending to directory user_copy
18/06/26  06:39:15 INFO util.AppendUtils: Using found partition 1
18/06/26  06:39:15 INFO tool.ImportTool: Incremental import complete! To run another incremental im
 all data following this import, supply the following arguments:
18/06/26  06:39:15 INFO tool.ImportTool:   --incremental append
18/06/26  06:39:15 INFO tool.ImportTool:   --check-column uid
18/06/26  06:39:15 INFO tool.ImportTool:   --last-value 5
18/06/26  06:39:15 INFO tool.ImportTool: (Consider saving this with 'sqoop job --create')
hadoop@7b1723229953:~$ hadoop fs -cat /sqoop/test/user/part-m-*
cat:  `/sqoop/test/user/part-m-*': No such file or directory
hadoop@7b1723229953:~$ hadoop fs -cat /sqoop/export/test/user_copy/part-m-*
1@zhangsan@22
2@lisi@23
3@wangwu@20
4@zhang1@24
5@zahng2@22
hadoop@7b1723229953:~$
```

(2)sqoop Export 的插入和更新。

```
$ sqoop export --connect jdbc:mysql://127.0.0.1/export_test --username root --password-file /user/hadoop/.password --table user_copy --export-dir /sqoop/export/test/user_copy --input-fields-terminated-by "@" -m 1 --update-key uid --update-mode allowinsert
```

说明：

--update-key ＜col-name＞更新参考的列名称，多个列名使用逗号分隔。

--update-mode ＜mode＞指定更新策略，包括 updateonly（默认）、allowinsert。

```
hadoop@7b1723229953:~$ sqoop export --connect jdbc:mysql://127.0.0.1/export_test --username root
rd-file /user/hadoop/.password --table user_copy --export-dir /sqoop/export/test/user_copy --input-
terminated-by '@' -m 1 --update-key uid --update-mode allowinsert
Warning: /hadoop/app/sqoop/../hbase does not exist! HBase imports will fail.
Please set $HBASE_HOME to the root of your HBase installation.
Warning: /hadoop/app/sqoop/../hcatalog does not exist! HCatalog jobs will fail.
Please set $HCAT_HOME to the root of your HCatalog installation.
Warning: /hadoop/app/sqoop/../accumulo does not exist! Accumulo imports will fail.
Please set $ACCUMULO_HOME to the root of your Accumulo installation.
Warning: /hadoop/app/sqoop/../zookeeper does not exist! Accumulo imports will fail.
Please set $ZOOKEEPER_HOME to the root of your Zookeeper installation.
18/06/26 06:40:42 INFO sqoop.Sqoop: Running Sqoop version: 1.4.6
18/06/26 06:40:43 INFO manager.MySQLManager: Preparing to use a MySQL streaming resultset.
18/06/26 06:40:43 INFO tool.CodeGenTool: Beginning code generation
18/06/26 06:40:43 INFO manager.SqlManager: Executing SQL statement: SELECT t.* FROM `user_copy` AS
 1
18/06/26 06:40:43 INFO manager.SqlManager: Executing SQL statement: SELECT t.* FROM `user_copy` AS
 1
18/06/26 06:40:43 INFO orm.CompilationManager: HADOOP_MAPRED_HOME is /hadoop/hadoop
Note: /tmp/sqoop-hadoop/compile/57f59c88ea56944d5e46ff14a52d7801/user_copy.java uses or overrides a
ated API.
Note: Recompile with -Xlint:deprecation for details.
18/06/26 06:40:44 INFO orm.CompilationManager: Writing jar file: /tmp/sqoop-hadoop/compile/57f59c8
d5e46ff14a52d7801/user_copy.jar
18/06/26 06:40:44 WARN manager.MySQLManager: MySQL Connector upsert functionality is using INSE
18/06/26 06:40:44 WARN manager.MySQLManager: DUPLICATE KEY UPDATE clause that relies on table
18/06/26 06:40:44 WARN manager.MySQLManager: Insert/update distinction is therefore independent
18/06/26 06:40:44 WARN manager.MySQLManager: names specified in --update-key parameter. Please
18/06/26 06:40:44 WARN manager.MySQLManager: documentation for additional limitations.
18/06/26 06:40:44 INFO mapreduce.ExportJobBase: Beginning export of user_copy
18/06/26 06:40:44 INFO Configuration.deprecation: mapred.jar is deprecated. Instead, use mapreduc
18/06/26 06:40:44 INFO Configuration.deprecation: mapred.reduce.tasks.speculative.execution is deprec
Instead, use mapreduce.reduce.speculative
18/06/26 06:40:44 INFO Configuration.deprecation: mapred.map.tasks.speculative.execution is deprec
stead, use mapreduce.map.speculative
```

```
        Total time spent by all map tasks (ms)=2500
        Total vcore-seconds taken by all map tasks=2500
        Total megabyte-seconds taken by all map tasks=2560000
    Map-Reduce Framework
        Map input records=5
        Map output records=5
        Input split bytes=222
        Spilled Records=0
        Failed Shuffles=0
        Merged Map outputs=0
        GC time elapsed (ms)=18
        CPU time spent (ms)=590
        Physical memory (bytes) snapshot=227577856
        Virtual memory (bytes) snapshot=891629568
        Total committed heap usage (bytes)=201326592
    File Input Format Counters
        Bytes Read=0
    File Output Format Counters
        Bytes Written=0
18/06/26 06:40:56 INFO mapreduce.ExportJobBase: Transferred 288 bytes in 11.6533 seconds (24.71
c)
18/06/26 06:40:56 INFO mapreduce.ExportJobBase: Exported 5 records.
hadoop@7b1723229953:~$
```

（3）导出后登录 MySQL 查看 user_copy 表中内容。

登录 MySQL，用户名为 root，密码为 root。

```
$ mysql -u root -p
Enter password:输入 root 回车即可
```

```
mysql> use export_test;
Database changed
```

查看 user_copy 表中的数据。

```
mysql> select * from user_copy;
```

退出 MySQL。

```
mysql> exit
```

```
mysql> use export_test;
Reading table information for completion of table and column names
You can turn off this feature to get a quicker startup with -A

Database changed
mysql> select * from user_copy;
+-----+----------+------+
| uid | name     | age  |
+-----+----------+------+
|   1 | zhangsan |   22 |
|   2 | lisi     |   23 |
|   3 | wangwu   |   20 |
|   4 | zhang1   |   24 |
|   5 | zahng2   |   22 |
+-----+----------+------+
5 rows in set (0.00 sec)

mysql>
```

由上图可看到每个 uid 相应的 age 已经由 100 岁又更新到了原来的值；hdfs 上新插入的数据也插入到了 user_copy 表中。

4）sqoop Export 应用场景——事务处理

(1) 登录 MySQL，删除数据库表 user_copy 中的内容。

登录 MySQL，用户名为 root，密码为 root。

```
$ mysql -u root -p
Enter password:输入 root 回车即可
```

使用 export_test 数据库。

```
mysql> use export_test;
Database changed
```

查看 user_copy 表中的数据。

```
mysql> select * from user_copy;
```

```
mysql> delete from user_copy;
Query OK, 2 rows affected (0.00 sec)
```

```
mysql> select * from user_copy;
Empty set (0.00 sec)
```

退出 MySQL。

```
mysql> exit
```

(2)将数据从 hdfs 导出。

```
$ sqoop export --connect jdbc:mysql://127.0.0.1/export_test  --username root --password-file /user/hadoop/.password --table user_copy --staging-table user_copy_tmp --clear-staging-table --export-dir /sqoop/export/test/user_copy --input-fields-terminated-by "@"
```

说明:

--staging-table <staging-table-name>在数据导出到数据库之前,数据临时存放的表名称,该参数是用来保证在数据导入关系数据库表的过程中事务安全性的,因为在导入的过程中可能会有多个事务,那么一个事务失败会影响到其他事务,比如导入的数据会出现错误或出现重复的记录等情况,那么通过该参数可以避免这种情况。创建一个与导入目标表同样的数据结构,保留该表为空在运行数据导入前,所有事务会将结果先存放在该表中,然后由该表通过一次事务将结果写入到目标表中。

--clear-staging-table 清除工作区中临时存放的数据。

这样执行会出现如下错误,需要提前创建临时表。

```
                Launched map tasks=3
                Data-local map tasks=3
                Total time spent by all maps in occupied slots (ms)=11366
                Total time spent by all reduces in occupied slots (ms)=0
                Total time spent by all map tasks (ms)=11366
                Total vcore-seconds taken by all map tasks=11366
                Total megabyte-seconds taken by all map tasks=11638784
        Map-Reduce Framework
                Map input records=5
                Map output records=5
                Input split bytes=587
                Spilled Records=0
                Failed Shuffles=0
                Merged Map outputs=0
                GC time elapsed (ms)=109
                CPU time spent (ms)=1870
                Physical memory (bytes) snapshot=704151552
                Virtual memory (bytes) snapshot=2683817984
                Total committed heap usage (bytes)=603979776
        File Input Format Counters
                Bytes Read=0
        File Output Format Counters
                Bytes Written=0
18/06/26 07:18:34 INFO mapreduce.ExportJobBase: Transferred 706 bytes in 13.575 seconds (52.007
18/06/26 07:18:34 INFO mapreduce.ExportJobBase: Exported 5 records.
18/06/26 07:18:34 INFO manager.SqlManager: Starting to migrate data from staging table to de
18/06/26 07:18:34 INFO manager.SqlManager: Migrated 5 records from `user_copy_tmp` to `user_cop
hadoop@7b1723329953:~$
```

(3)创建临时表 user_copy_tmp。

登录 MySQL,用户名为 root,密码为 root。

```
$ mysql -u root -p
Enter password:输入 root 回车即可
```

使用 export_test 数据库。

```
mysql> use export_test;
Database changed
```

创建 user_copy_tmp 数据库表。

```
mysql> create table user_copy_tmp(uid int auto_increment primary key,name varchar(20) not null,age int(5));
Query OK, 0 rows affected (0.01 sec)
```

退出 MySQL。

```
mysql> exit
```

(4)再次将数据从 hdfs 导出。

```
$ sqoop export --connect jdbc:mysql://127.0.0.1/export_test --username root --password-file /user/hadoop/.password --table user_copy --staging-table user_copy_tmp --clear-staging-table --export-dir /sqoop/export/test/user_copy --input-fields-terminated-by "@"
```

(5)导出后登录 MySQL 查看 user_copy 表中内容。

登录 MySQL,用户名为 root,密码为 root。

```
$ mysql -u root -p
Enter password:输入 root 回车即可
```

```
mysql> use export_test;
Database changed
```

查看 user_copy 表中的数据。

```
mysql> select * from user_copy;
```

查看 user_copy 表中的数据。

```
mysql> select * from user_copy_tmp;
```

退出 MySQL。

```
mysql> exit
```

由上图可知,目标表中已经导入了数据,而临时表已经被清除了临时存放的数据。

5)sqoop Export 应用场景——字段不对应问题

(1)登录 MySQL,删除数据库表 user_copy 中的内容。

登录 MySQL,用户名为 root,密码为 root。

```
$ mysql -u root -p
Enter password: 输入 root 回车即可
```

使用 export_test 数据库。

```
mysql> use export_test;
Database changed
```

查看 user_copy 表中的数据。

```
mysql> select * from user_copy;
```

```
mysql> delete from user_copy;
Query OK, 2 rows affected (0.00 sec)
```

```
mysql> select * from user_copy;
Empty set (0.00 sec)
```

退出 MySQL。

```
mysql> exit
```

(2)选择 user 表的 name、age 两个字段导出来。

```
$ sqoop import --connect jdbc:mysql://127.0.0.1/export_test --username root --password-file /user/hadoop/.password --table user --columns name,age --target-dir /sqoop/export/test/user_copy --delete-target-dir -m 1 --fields-terminated-by "@ "
```

```
$ hadoop fs -cat /sqoop/export/test/user_copy/part-m-*
```

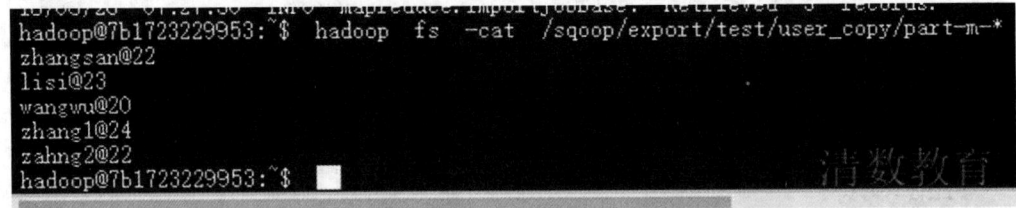

(3)将 hdfs 上数据导出。

```
$ sqoop export --connect jdbc:mysql://127.0.0.1/export_test --username root --password-file /user/hadoop/.password --table user_copy --columns name,age --export-dir /sqoop/export/test/user_copy --input-fields-terminated-by "@ " -m 1
```

说明：

--columns <col,col,col…> 从表中导出指定的一组列的数据。

(4)导出后登录 MySQL 查看 user_copy 表中内容。

登录 MySQL,用户名为 root,密码为 root。

```
$ mysql -u root -p
Enter password:输入 root 回车即可
```

```
mysql> use export_test;
Database changed
```

查看 user_copy 表中的数据。

```
mysql> select * from user_copy;
```

退出 MySQL。

```
mysql> exit
hadoop-env
```

```
mysql> use export_test;
Reading table information for completion of table and column names
You can turn off this feature to get a quicker startup with -A

Database changed
mysql> select * from user_copy;
+-----+----------+------+
| uid | name     | age  |
+-----+----------+------+
|   6 | zhangsan |   22 |
|   7 | lisi     |   23 |
|   8 | wangwu   |   20 |
|   9 | zhang1   |   24 |
|  10 | zahng2   |   22 |
+-----+----------+------+
5 rows in set (0.00 sec)

mysql>
```

因为 user_copy 的主键 uid 为自增,且之前插入了 1~5 的数据,所以这里从 6 开始自增。

第六章 商业大数据挖掘方法

实验10 大数据挖掘
——电子商务数据的逻辑回归模型挖掘实验

一、实验介绍

1. 实验内容

本实验使用 pyspark 工具来进行逻辑回归的分类预测问题,逻辑回归是一类最为常用的有监督的机器学习模型,它具有良好的可解释性,在很多场景下的预测效果非常好。

2. 实验目标

掌握使用 pyspark 进行逻辑回归预测的方法。
熟悉逻辑回归的基本原理。

3. 算法介绍

逻辑回归(Logistic Regression)是一类分类问题,用于二分类问题,如"预测泰坦尼克号中乘客是否能幸存""某位客户是否会违约"等问题。

该算法是从线性回归的基础上演化而来,线性回归中的预测值的取值范围为 $(-\infty, +\infty)$,将该预测值代入逻辑函数:

$$g(z) = \frac{1}{(1-exp(-1))}$$

即可将预测值的取值范围规约到 (0,1) 之间。然后通过设定阈值(threshold)得到最终的分类结果。

二、实验步骤

```
from pyspark.sql import SparkSession
from pyspark.ml.classification import LogisticRegression
from pyspark.ml.evaluation import MulticlassClassificationEvaluator
```

```
# 创建一个任务,设置任务名称
spark = SparkSession.builder.appName('LogisticRegressionExercise').getOrCreate()
```

```
# 加载数据。还是 libsvm 类型的数据
data = spark.read.format('libsvm').load('/home/ds/data/DW/lr_libsvm_data.txt')
data.show(5)
```

输出结果如下:

```
+-----+--------------------+--------------------+--------------------+----------+
|label|            features|       rawPrediction|         probability|prediction|
+-----+--------------------+--------------------+--------------------+----------+
|  0.0|(692,[100,101,102...|[9.59901243946602...|[0.99993220894018...|       0.0|
|  0.0|(692,[122,123,148...|[14.2257524554819...|[0.99999933651070...|       0.0|
|  0.0|(692,[123,124,125...|[30.8960369395607...|[0.99999999999996...|       0.0|
|  0.0|(692,[123,124,125...|[19.2328538745945...|[0.99999999556107...|       0.0|
|  0.0|(692,[124,125,126...|[29.8960300630719...|[0.99999999999989...|       0.0|
+-----+--------------------+--------------------+--------------------+----------+
only showing top 5 rows
```

```
# 构建一个评估器,前面实验多次用到
evaluator = MulticlassClassificationEvaluator(predictionCol='prediction',labelCol
='label',metricName='accuracy')
```

```
# 计算准确度
accuracy = evaluator.evaluate(prediction)
print(accuracy)
```

计算结果如下:

```
1.0
```

```
spark.stop()
```

三、练习题

(1) 逻辑回归用来解决分类任务还是回归任务?

逻辑回归虽然叫作回归,但是其本值是一种分类算法,它通过函数将预测值进行映射,从而得到一个分类概率,然后得到最终的分类结果。

(2) 解释回归模型中"threshold"参数的含义。

"threshold"是分类阈值,在本实验中,我们将此值设置为0.5,表明如果结果的预测值大于0.5,则将该条记录归为第一类;如果小于0.5,则将该条记录归为另一类。

实验 11　大数据挖掘
——电子商务数据的决策树分类模型挖掘实验

一、实验介绍

1. 实验内容

决策树是最常使用到的数据挖掘算法之一,我们经常使用决策树处理分类问题。本实验使用 pyspark 进行决策树回归模型的练习。

2. 实验目标

了解三种常用的决策树算法的基本原理。

掌握使用 pyspark 进行决策树分类的使用方法。

理解 libsvm 格式的数据表现形式。

3. 算法介绍

决策树是一类常见的机器学习算法。以二分类问题为例,我们希望从给定的训练数据集中学得一个模型用以对新的数据进行分类。样本一般具有很多个特征,有的特征对分类起重要作用,而有的特征对分类的作用很小。例如决定一个人是否贷款,这个人的信用记录、收入等就是主要的判断依据,而性别、年龄等则是次要的判断依据。决策树的构建过程,就是根据特征对结果的决定程度,先选择决定性程度高的特征分类,再使用决定程度低的特征进行分类,这样就会构建出一个决策树,这棵树就是我们用来进行分类的模型。

主要的决策树算法包括 ID3,C4.5,CART。

ID3 把信息增益作为划分的标准。我们希望决策树的分支节点所包含的样本尽可能属于同一个类别,即节点的"纯度"越来越高。在这种情况下,取值较多的特征的信息增益比较大,更容易被用作划分的特征。而且该算法只能用于离散型数据。

C4.5 算法与 ID3 算法类似,区别在于选择使用信息增益比作为划分的标准,这种方法会比 ID3 算法更加科学,而且也可用于连续性变量。

CART 算法选择使用"基尼指数"(Gini Index)来划分特征。基尼指数越低,说明数据集的纯度越高。因此选择那个使得划分后基尼指数最小的属性作为最优化分属性。

二、实验过程

libsvm 数据形式 Label 1:Value 2:Value

Label:数据类别的标识。对于分类问题,该值表示数据的类别,即该条记录所属的类别(如 0,1,2 等);对于回归问题,该值指的是目标值。

Value:要训练的数据,即记录的特征值,每个数据之间用空格隔开。如果特征值为0,特征冒号前面的序号可以不连续,如:

1 2:3 5:6 9:1

该数据表示:这条记录属于第1类,第二个位置的值为3,第五个位置的数据为6,第九个位置的数据为1,其他位置的数据为0。

```
# 观察一下数据的前三行
! head -3 '/home/ds/data/DW/dt_libsvm_data.txt'
```

0 128:51 129:159 130:253 131:159 132:50 155:48 156:238 157:252 158:252 159:252 160:237 182:54 183:227 184:253 185:252 186:239 187:233 188:252 189:57 190:6 208:10 209:60 210:224 211:252 212:253 213:252 214:202 215:84 216:252 217:253 218:122 236:163 237:252 238:252 239:252 240:253 241:252 242:252 243:96 244:189 245:253 246:167 263:51 264:238 265:253 266:253 267:190 268:114 269:253 270:228 271:47 272:79 273:255 274:168 290:48 291:238 292:252 293:252 294:179 295:12 296:75 297:121 298:21 301:253 302:243 303:50 317:38 318:165 319:253 320:233 321:208 322:84 329:253 330:252 331:165 344:7 345:178 346:252 347:240 348:71 349:19 350:28 357:253 358:252 359:195 372:57 373:252 374:252 375:63 385:253 386:252 387:195 400:198 401:253 402:190 413:255 414:253 415:196 427:76 428:246 429:252 430:112 441:253 442:252 443:148 455:85 456:252 457:230 458:25 467:7 468:135 469:253 470:186 471:12 483:85 484:252 485:223 494:7 495:131 496:252 497:225 498:71 511:85 512:252 513:145 521:48 522:165 523:252 524:173 539:86 540:253 541:225 548:114 549:238 550:253 551:162 567:85 568:252 569:249 570:146 571:48 572:29 573:85 574:178 575:225 576:253 577:223 578:167 579:56 595:85 596:252 597:252 598:252 599:229 600:215 601:252 602:252 603:252 604:196 605:130 623:28 624:199 625:252 626:252 627:253 628:252 629:252 630:233 631:145 652:25 653:128 654:252 655:253 656:252 657:141 658:37
1 159:124 160:253 161:255 162:63 186:96 187:244 188:251 189:253 190:62 214:127 215:251 216:251 217:253 218:62 241:68 242:236 243:251 244:211 245:31 246:8 268:60 269:228 270:251 271:251 272:94 296:155 297:253 298:253 299:189 323:20 324:253 325:251 326:235 327:66 350:32 351:205 352:253 353:251 354:126 378:104 379:251 380:253 381:184 382:15 405:80 406:240 407:251 408:193 409:23 432:32 433:253 434:253 435:253 436:159 460:151 461:251 462:251 463:251 464:39 487:48 488:221 489:251 490:251 491:172 515:234 516:251 517:251 518:196 519:12 543:253 544:251 545:251 546:89 570:159 571:255 572:253 573:253 574:31 597:48 598:228 599:253 600:247 601:140 602:8 625:64 626:251 627:253 628:220 653:64 654:251 655:253 656:220 681:24 682:193 683:253 684:220

1 125:145 126:255 127:211 128:31 152:32 153:237 154:253 155:252 156:71 180:11 181:
175 182:253 183:252 184:71 209:144 210:253 211:252 212:71 236:16 237:191 238:
253 239:252 240:71 264:26 265:221 266:253 267:252 268:124 269:31 293:125 294:
253 295:252 296:252 297:108 322:253 323:252 324:252 325:108 350:255 351:253 352:
253 353:108 378:253 379:252 380:252 381:108 406:253 407:252 408:252 409:108 434:
253 435:252 436:252 437:108 462:255 463:253 464:253 465:170 490:253 491:252 492:
252 493:252 494:42 518:149 519:252 520:252 521:252 522:144 546:109 547:252 548:
252 549:252 550:144 575:218 576:253 577:253 578:255 579:35 603:175 604:252 605:
252 606:253 607:35 631:73 632:252 633:252 634:253 635:35 659:31 660:211 661:252 662:
253 663:35

```
# 导入相关程序包
# 导入 SparkSession 模块,该模块为 spark 功能的入口
from pyspark.sql import SparkSession
# 导入特征处理的模块
from pyspark.ml.feature import StringIndexer,VectorIndexer
# 导入分类器
from pyspark.ml.classification import DecisionTreeClassifier
# 导入管道模块
from pyspark.ml import Pipeline
# 导入模型评估模块
from pyspark.ml.evaluation import MulticlassClassificationEvaluator
```

```
# 给该任务一个名字
spark = SparkSession.builder.appName('Decision Tree classification model').getOrCreate()
```

```
# 读入数据,libsvm 格式的数据自动区分特征和标签值。
data = spark.read.format('libsvm').load('/home/ds/data/DW/dt_libsvm_data.txt')
```

```
# 显示前 5 行,观看一下数据。
data.show(n = 5)
```

输出结果如下:

```
+----+--------------------+
|label|            features|
+----+--------------------+
| 0.0|(692,[127,128,129...|
| 1.0|(692,[158,159,160...|
| 1.0|(692,[124,125,126...|
| 1.0|(692,[152,153,154...|
| 1.0|(692,[151,152,153...|
+----+--------------------+
only showing top 5 rows
```

```
'''
对标签值进行处理,将类别标注为(0,n-1),默认按照出现的频数进行标注,数量最多的类别标注为0,依次类推。
输入列为'label',输出列为'indexedLabel'
对数据进行拟合
'''
labelIndexer= StringIndexer(inputCol= 'label',outputCol= 'indexedLabel').fit(data)
```

```
'''
对特征列进行处理,能够自动识别类别型的特征。
在此我们指定'maxCategories'的值为4,表示当某一特征中数值的类别超过4时,自动识别这一列为连续型变量,否则为
类别型变量。然后将类别型的特征转换为(0,n-1)。
'''
featureIndexer = VectorIndexer(inputCol= 'features',outputCol= 'indexedFeatures',maxCategories= 4).fit(data)
```

```
# 构建决策树模型,指定特征列和标签列,设置预测值列的名称
dt = DecisionTreeClassifier(featuresCol= 'indexedFeatures',labelCol= 'indexedLabel',predictionCol= 'predictedLabel')
```

```
# 构建一个管道,将以上三个操作进行整合,这样可以直接方便的进行调用。
pipeline = Pipeline(stages = [labelIndexer,featureIndexer,dt])
```

```python
# 切分训练集和测试集,因为数据格式为 Libsvm,所以不用认为指定特征列和标签列
(trainingData,testingData) = data.randomSplit([0.7,0.3])
```

```python
# 拟合训练集
model = pipeline.fit(trainingData)
```

```python
# 在测试集上进行预测,得到预测结果
prediction = model.transform(testingData)
```

```python
# 构建一个评估器,labelCol 表示真实值的列,predictionCol 表示预测值,评估标准为准确度。
evaluator = MulticlassClassificationEvaluator(labelCol = 'indexedLabel',predic-
tionCol= 'predictedLabel',metricName= 'accuracy')
# 对预测结果进行评估
accuracy = evaluator.evaluate(prediction)
```

```python
# 测试准确率为 92.86%
print('Test accuracy is {0:.4f}'.format(accuracy))
```

测试准确率:

```
Test accuracy is 1.0000
```

```python
# 停止该任务,释放资源。
spark.stop()
```

三、实验总结

(1)构建一个 SparkSession,给一个任务名。

(2)读入数据。

(3)分别对标签列和特征列进行处理。

(4)构建一个分类器。

(5)组装管道。

(6)进行训练集、测试集切分。

(7)拟合训练集,在测试集上进行预测。

(8)评估预测效果。

(9)停止任务。

四、练习题

(1)常见的决策树算法有几类？每类之间的区别是什么？

常见的决策树算法有 3 类。ID3 算法、C4.5 算法、CART 算法。

ID3 算法采用信息增益作为划分特征的标准。

C4.5 算法在 ID3 算法的基础上做了改进,采用信息增益率作为划分特征的标准,避免了类别过多的特征对划分结果的影响。

CART 算法则采用基尼指数作为划分特征的标准。

(2)在 pyspark 中,使用什么方法可以将类别型特征标记为从 0 至 n-1 的数字？使用什么方法可以划分类别型特征和连续型特征？

使用 StringIndexer 可以将类别型特征标记为数字,出现频数最多的特征会被标记为 0。

使用 VectorIndexer 可以识别类别型特征。

实验 12 大数据挖掘
——利用 Apriori 算法进行电子商务数据的关联规则挖掘实验

一、实验介绍

1. 实验内容

关联规则挖掘广泛应用于电子商务、零售等行业。通过分析哪些商品经常在一起被购买,可以帮助商家了解消费者的购物行为。这种从数据海样中抽取的知识可以用于商品定价、市场促销、存货管理等环节,从大规模数据集中寻找物品间的隐含关系被称作关联分析(association analysis)或者关联规则学习(association rule learning)。

关联规则挖掘的目标有两个:
(1)找出频繁项集。
(2)找出关联规则。

本实验首先将简要介绍 Apriori 算法,然后作为对比,介绍另外一种更为高效的关联规则挖掘方法(FP-growth)。

2. 实验目标

(1)了解 Apriori 算法与 FP-Growth 算法的区别。
(2)掌握使用 pyspark 进行关联规则挖掘的方法。
(3)理解输入参数的含义,即支持度和置信度的含义。
(4)理解实验结果的含义,即频繁项集、关联规则的含义。

3. 算法介绍

1)Apriori 算法

Apriori 算法是一种发现频繁项集的方法。它的核心思想是:如果一个项集是不频繁的,那么所有包含该项集的超集也是不频繁的。该算法有两个输入参数,一是最小支持度,二是最小置信度。首先它会生成所有单个物品的项集列表。然后扫描整份数据,计算哪些项集满足设置的最小支持度的要求。那些不满足最小支持度的项集就会被去掉。接着对剩下的集合进行组合,生成包含两个元素的集合,再扫描整份记录,计算每个项集的支持度,去除不满足最小支持度的项集,依此类推,直到所有项集被去掉。

Apriori 算法的缺点在于:每次增加频繁项集中元素的数量,Apriori 算法都会重新扫描整份数据集。当数据集很大时,这显著会降低算法的运行速度。

2)FP-Growth 算法

它是基于 Apriori 算法构建,但在完成相同任务时,采用了一种不同的方法,这里首先将数据存储在一个特定的 FP 树的结构上,然后进行频繁项集挖掘,这种做法使得 FP-Growth 算法的执行效率要远高于 Apriori 算法,通常性能要好两个数量级以上。FP-Growth 算法只需要对数据库进行两次扫描,而 Apriori 算法对于每个潜在的频繁项集都会扫描数据集以判定该模式是否频繁,因此 FP-Growth 算法的执行速度要远高于 Apriori 算法。

3)相关参数

(1)关联规则:用于表示数据内隐含的关联性,一般用 X 表示先决条件,Y 表示关联结果。

(2)支持度(Support):所有项集中$\{X,Y\}$出现的可能性。

(3)置信度(Confidence):先决条件 X 发生的条件下,关联结果 Y 发生的概率。

二、实验步骤

数据介绍

(1)该数据来源于某电商网站上消费者的购物记录,共包含 131 209 条购物记录。

(2)每行代表一个购物记录,记录中的数字代表消费者所购买的商品。

(3)数据已脱密,因此每种商品用数字表示。

```
# 首先观看一下数据前 5 行的格式
! head -5 '/home/ds/data/DW/fp_growth.txt'
```

```
# 导入相关工具包
# 导入 SparkSession,SparkSession 是 spark 操作的入口
from pyspark.sql import SparkSession
# 导入 fp-growth 模块
from pyspark.ml.fpm import FPGrowth
# 导入数据类型变换模块
from pyspark.sql.types import *
```

```
# 因为 spark 是在分布式集群上执行,所以首先需要给一个名字,标注一下任务
spark = SparkSession.builder.appName('fpgrowth mining').getOrCreate()
```

```
# 读入文件,读入的格式为 rdd
lines = spark.sparkContext.textFile('/home/ds/data/DW/fp_growth.txt')
```

```
# 将每行数据按照逗号进行分隔
parts = lines.map(lambda x : x.strip().split(","))
```

```
# 将每行数据组成一个包含两个元素的 tuple,第一个元素为 id,第二个元素为数据(按照空格进行分隔)
trans = parts.map(lambda p :(p[0],p[1].strip().split(" ")))
# 设置 DataFrame 的模式,即列名和每列的数据类型,第一列为字符串类型,第二列为序列型
fields = [StructField('id', StringType(), True),StructField('item_name', ArrayType
(StringType()), True)]
schema = StructType(fields)


# 将 RDD 转换为 DataFrame
data = spark.createDataFrame(trans,schema)


# 查看 data,show() 默认显示前 20 行。功能于 pandas 中的 head() 一致
data.show()
```

输出结果如下:

```
+---+--------------------+
| id|           item_name|
+---+--------------------+
|  0|[49302, 11109, 10...|
|  1|[39612, 19660, 49...|
|  2|[11913, 18159, 44...|
|  3|[20574, 30391, 40...|
|  4|[8859, 19731, 436...|
|  5|[27104, 21174, 41...|
|  6|[18394, 37766, 13...|
|  7|[1194, 5578, 3815...|
|  8|[28199, 24852, 29...|
|  9|[33000, 11361, 27...|
| 10|[12078, 6184, 324...|
| 11|[18196, 34229, 48...|
| 12|[20082, 24852, 47...|
| 13|[21137, 27344, 42...|
| 14|            [45683]|
| 15|[21137, 41220, 15...|
| 16|[47482, 43335, 16...|
| 17|[14992, 21405, 11...|
```

```
|18|[48070, 24852, 23...|
|19|         [8013, 46149]|
+---+--------------------+
only showing top 20 rows
```

```
# 查看数据总量
data.count()
```

数据总量为:131 209

```
# 构建一个 fpgrowth 的对象,需要进行操作的列为'item_name',最小支持度为 0.01,最小置信度设置
为 0.01
fpGrowth = FPGrowth(itemsCol= 'item_name',minSupport= 0.01,minConfidence= 0.01)
# 使用该对象拟合数据
model = fpGrowth.fit(data)
# 显示频繁项集
model.freqItemsets.show()
# 结果解读:第一列为频繁项集,第二列为出现的频次
```

输出结果如下:

```
+--------------+----+
|         items|freq|
+--------------+----+
|        [5025]|1445|
|       [11777]|1493|
|       [37067]|2332|
|       [20114]|1899|
|       [19057]|2891|
|       [22035]|1993|
|       [26209]|6033|
|[26209, 47626]|1595|
|[26209, 24852]|1331|
|       [43961]|2460|
|       [43352]|3279|
|       [38739]|1633|
```

```
|          [20995]| 1361|
|          [27344]| 1788|
|          [19660]| 2225|
|          [28985]| 2627|
|           [4605]| 3762|
|          [21137]|10894|
|[21137, 13176]| 3074|
|[21137, 24852]| 2174|
+--------------+-----+
only showing top 20 rows
```

# 显示关联规则,第一列为前项,第二列为后项,'如果...就...'最后一列为置信度。
model.associationRules.show()

输出结果如下:

```
+----------+----------+-------------------+
|antecedent|consequent|         confidence|
+----------+----------+-------------------+
|   [21903]|   [47766]|0.14329517579721995|
|   [21903]|   [21137]|0.16751839738348323|
|   [21903]|   [13176]| 0.2285363859362224|
|   [21903]|   [24852]| 0.2044153720359771|
|   [16797]|   [24852]|0.29996920234062213|
|   [47766]|   [47626]|0.18207585369145635|
|   [47766]|   [21903]|0.18922931569712512|
|   [47766]|   [24852]| 0.2990956944256985|
|   [21137]|   [13176]|0.28217367358178813|
|   [21137]|   [24852]|0.19955939049017807|
|   [21137]|   [47209]| 0.1412704240866532|
|   [21137]|   [27966]|0.15329539195887645|
|   [21137]|   [21903]|0.15044978887460989|
|   [47209]|   [21137]|0.21102426984779926|
|   [47209]|   [13176]|0.33182503770739064|
|   [26209]|   [47626]| 0.264379247472236|
|   [26209]|   [24852]|0.22061992375269351|
|   [27966]|   [21137]| 0.3011179228272629|
```

```
|   [27966]|    [13176]|0.32095203750450774|
|   [47626]|    [26209]|0.196066379840196668|
+----------+----------+-------------------+
only showing top 20 rows
```

```
# 符合条件的关联规则的数量
model.associationRules.count()
```

符合条件的关联规则的数量为:32

```
# 在所有任务执行完成之后,停止该任务,释放资源。
spark.stop()
```

三、练习题

(1)掌握使用 head 命令查看文件前几行的便捷方法。

! head -5 ′/home/ds/data/DW/fp_growth.txt′

(2)在使用 pyspark 执行任务时,任务的第一步和最后一步分别是什么?

第一步是利用 SparkSession 设置一个 spark 任务,并且给定一个任务名称。

最后一步是停止 spark 任务,释放资源。

(3)Fpgrowth 算法和 Apriori 算法相比,有何显著的优点?

Fpgrowth 算法只需对整个数据集扫描两次,即可得到所有满足条件的频繁项集。而 Apriori 算法在计算过程中,每次频繁项集的个数增加一个,就需要扫描一次数据集,效率比 Fpgrowth 算法低很多。

实验 13　大数据挖掘
——利用 K-means 算法进行数据挖掘实验

一、实验介绍

1. 实验内容

K-means 算法是一类最常用的无监督学习算法,该方法常用于数据的初步分析阶段,通过该方法可以得知数据大概可分为几个类别,便于对数据有初步的认识。本实验使用 pyspark 来进行聚类分析。

2. 实验目标

掌握使用 pyspark 进行 Kmeans 算法的流程。
了解 K-means 算法的基本原理。

3. 算法介绍

K-means 算法是发现给定数据集中 k 个簇的算法。该算法中簇的个数 k 由用户指定,每一个簇通过其质心,即簇中所有点的中心来描述。

该算法的工作流程是这样的。首先,随机指定 k 个点作为初始质心,然后将数据集中的每个点分配到一个簇中(通常来讲是计算欧式距离),即将每个点分配到距离其最近的质心。然后每个簇的质心更新为该簇所有点的平均值。依此类推,直到簇不发生变化,算法停止。

二、实验步骤

```
from pyspark.sql import SparkSession
from pyspark.ml.clustering import KMeans
from pyspark.ml.feature import VectorAssembler
from pyspark.sql.types import IntegerType,DoubleType
```

```
# 创建一个任务,设置任务名称
spark = SparkSession.builder.appName('kmeans exercise').getOrCreate()
```

```
# 创建一个任务,设置任务名称
spark = SparkSession.builder.appName('kmeans exercise').getOrCreate()
```

输出结果如下：

_c0	Private	Apps	Accept	Enroll	Top10perc	Top25perc	F.Undergrad	P.Undergrad	Outstate	Room.Board	Books	Personal	PhD	Terminal	S.F.Ratio	perc.alumni	Expend	Grad.Rate
Abilene Christian...	Yes	1660	1232	721	23	52	2885	537	7440	3300	450	2200	70	78	18.1	12	7041	60
Adelphi University	Yes	2186	1924	512	16	29	2683	1227	12280	6450	750	1500	29	30	12.2	16	10527	56
Adrian College	Yes	1428	1097	336	22	50	1036	99	11250	3750	400	1165	53	66	12.9	30	8735	54
Agnes Scott College	Yes	417	349	137	60	89	510	63	12960	5450	450	875	92	97	7.7	37	19016	59
Alaska Pacific Un...	Yes	193	146	55	16	44	249	869	7560	4120	800	1500	76	72	11.9	2	10922	15

only showing top 5 rows

```
# 查看每个特征的数据类型
data.printSchema
# 所有特征均为字符串型，因此需要将其改为数值型
```

<bound method DataFrame.printSchema of DataFrame[_c0: string, Private: string, Apps: string, Accept: string, Enroll: string, Top10perc: string, Top25perc: string, F.Undergrad: string, P.Undergrad: string, Outstate: string, Room.Board: string, Books: string, Personal: string, PhD: string, Terminal: string, S.F.Ratio: string, perc.alumni: string, Expend: string, Grad.Rate: string]>

```
# 将每列的格式改为数值型特征
data = data.withColumn('Apps',data['Apps'].cast(IntegerType()))
```

```
data = data.withColumn('Accept',data['Accept'].cast(IntegerType()))
data = data.withColumn('Enroll',data['Enroll'].cast(IntegerType()))
data = data.withColumn('Top10perc',data['Top10perc'].cast(IntegerType()))
data = data.withColumn('Top25perc',data['Top25perc'].cast(IntegerType()))
data = data.withColumn('Outstate',data['Outstate'].cast(IntegerType()))
data= data.withColumn('Books',data['Books'].cast(IntegerType()))
data = data.withColumn('Personal',data['Personal'].cast(IntegerType()))
data = data.withColumn('PhD',data['PhD'].cast(IntegerType()))
data = data.withColumn('Terminal',data['Terminal'].cast(IntegerType()))
data = data.withColumn('Expend',data['Expend'].cast(IntegerType()))
```

```
# 因列名中含有点(.),因此使用反引号来进行引用
data = data.withColumn('F_Undergrad',data['`F.Undergrad`'].cast(IntegerType()))
data = data.withColumn('P_Undergrad',data['`P.Undergrad`'].cast(IntegerType()))
data = data.withColumn('Room_Board',data['`Room.Board`'].cast(IntegerType()))
data = data.withColumn('perc_alumni',data['`perc.alumni`'].cast(IntegerType()))
data = data.withColumn('Grad_Rate',data['`Grad.Rate`'].cast(IntegerType()))
```

```
# 将该列转换为浮点型
data = data.withColumn('S_F_Ratio',data['`S.F.Ratio`'].cast(DoubleType()))
```

```
# 重新查看数据类型
data.printSchema
```

<bound method DataFrame.printSchema of DataFrame[_c0：string, Private：string, Apps：int, Accept：int, Enroll：int, Top10perc：int, Top25perc：int, F.Undergrad：string, P.Undergrad：string, Outstate：int, Room.Board：string, Books：int, Personal：int, PhD：int, Terminal：int, S.F.Ratio：string, perc.alumni：string, Expend：int, Grad.Rate：string, F_Undergrad：int, P_Undergrad：int, Room_Board：int, perc_alumni：int, Grad_Rate：int, S_F_Ratio：double]>

```
# 将用于聚类的特征进行组装
assember = VectorAssembler(inputCols=['Apps','Accept','Enroll','Top10perc','Top25perc',"F_Undergrad",'P_Undergrad',
```

```
    'Outstate','Room_Board','Books','Personal','PhD','Terminal','S_F_Ratio','perc_
alumni','Expend','Grad_Rate'],
                        outputCol = 'features')
data1 = assember.transform(data)
data1.show(5)
```

输出结果如下:

```
+-------------------+-------+----+------+------+---------+---------+-----------+----------+--------+----------+-----+--------+---+--------+--------+----------+------+--------+--------+----------+--------------------+
|                 _c0|Private|Apps|Accept|Enroll|Top10perc|Top25perc|F.Undergrad|P.Undergrad|Outstate|Room.Board|Books|Personal|PhD|Terminal|S.F.Ratio|perc.alumni|Expend|Grad.Rate|F_Undergrad|P_Undergrad|Room_Board|perc_alumni|Grad_Rate|S_F_Ratio|            features|
+-------------------+-------+----+------+------+---------+---------+-----------+----------+--------+----------+-----+--------+---+--------+--------+----------+------+--------+--------+----------+--------------------+
|Abilene Christian...|    Yes|1660|  1232|   721|       23|       52|       2885|       537|    7440|      3300|  450|    2200| 70|      78|    18.1|        12|  7041|      60|    2885|     537|      3300|        12|       60|     18.1|[1660.0,1232.0,72...|
| Adelphi University|    Yes|2186|  1924|   512|       16|       29|       2683|      1227|   12280|      6450|  750|    1500| 29|      30|    12.2|        16| 10527|      56|    2683|    1227|      6450|        16|       56|     12.2|[2186.0,1924.0,51...|
|     Adrian College|    Yes|1428|  1097|   336|       22|       50|       1036|        99|   11250|      3750|  400|    1165| 53|      66|    12.9|        30|  8735|      54|    1036|      99|      3750|        30|       54|     12.9|[1428.0,1097.0,33...|
|Agnes Scott College|    Yes| 417|   349|   137|       60|       89|        510|        63|   12960|      5450|  450|     875| 92|      97|     7.7|        37| 19016|      59|     510|      63|      5450|        37|       59|      7.7|[417.0,349.0,137....|
|Alaska Pacific Un...|    Yes| 193|   146|    55|       16|       44|        249|       869|    7560|      4120|  800|    1500| 76|      72|    11.9|         2| 10922|      15|     249|     869|      4120|         2|       15|     11.9|[193.0,146.0,55.0...|
+-------------------+-------+----+------+------+---------+---------+-----------+----------+--------+----------+-----+--------+---+--------+--------+----------+------+--------+--------+----------+--------------------+
only showing top 5 rows
```

```
# 构建聚类模型,设置类别数为 2,结果输出在 prediction 列
kmeans = KMeans(featuresCol= 'features',predictionCol= 'prediction',k= 2)
```

```
# 拟合数据
model = kmeans.fit(data1)
```

```
# 进行聚类
predictions = model.transform(data1)
```

```
# 查看聚类中心
centers = model.clusterCenters()
for center in centers:
    print(center)
```

聚类中心为:

```
[  1.03631389e+ 04   6.55089815e+ 03   2.56972222e+ 03   4.14907407e+ 01
   7.02037037e+ 01   1.30619352e+ 04   2.46486111e+ 03   1.07191759e+ 04
   4.64347222e+ 03   5.95212963e+ 02   1.71420370e+ 03   8.63981481e+ 01
 9.13333333e+ 01   1.40277778e+ 01   2.00740741e+ 01   1.41705000e+ 04
   6.75925926e+ 01]
[  1813.23467862   1287.16591928    491.04484305     25.30941704
     53.47085202   2188.54857997    595.45889387   10395.70852018
   4311.36472347    541.98206278   1280.33632287     70.44245142
     77.82511211     14.09970105     23.17488789   8932.04633782
     65.11958146]
```

```
# 停止任务
spark.stop()
```

三、练习题

(1)K-means算法中,需要提前指定的参数是什么?该参数该如何选择?
分类的簇数 k。

该参数 k 需要由实验人员自行设定。k 值不同,聚类结果也不相同。在实际的场景中,一般 k 值需要多次尝试,才能得到一个较好的取值。另外,该参数的设定很多时候会向该领域的专业人士请教,由其来进行指定。

(2)请复述 K-means 算法的流程。

参照算法介绍部分。

实验 14　大数据挖掘实战案例
——利用大数据挖掘实现电影广告的精准营销

一、实验介绍

1. 实验内容

精准推荐是大数据时代的典型应用,诸如"今日头条"中的新闻推荐,"网易云音乐"中的音乐推荐等场景,其实背后都运用了精准推荐的技术。本实验通过使用 pyspark 来实现协同过滤算法,以此来实现电影的推荐。

2. 算法介绍

协同过滤算法是一种基于兴趣相同的用户或者项目进行推荐的算法。它的理念很简单,即根据与目标用户兴趣相同的用户的偏好信息来推荐。以电影推荐为例,当你不知道看什么电影时,肯定会向与自己兴趣相同的朋友询问,看看有没有什么好的电影推荐。这其实就是协同过滤算法的核心理念。协同过滤通过在海量的用户中发掘与你兴趣类似的用户,然后依据他们的兴趣得到一个推荐列表,再将这个列表展示给你。

二、实验要求

掌握协同过滤的核心理念。
熟练使用 pyspark 实现协同过滤算法。
能够熟练使用 pyspark 进行数据读取、格式转换、模型构建、结果评估等过程,不再依赖查找文档。

三、实验步骤

```
# 导入相关包
from pyspark.ml.evaluation import RegressionEvaluator
from pyspark.ml.recommendation import ALS
from pyspark.sql import SparkSession
from pyspark.sql.types import IntegerType,DoubleType
```

```
# 创建任务,给定任务名称
spark = SparkSession.builder.appName('movie recommendation').getOrCreate()
```

```
# 读入数据,该数据为电影评分数据,4列分别为用户ID,电影ID,电影评分,时间戳.
data = spark.read.format('com.databricks.spark.csv').options(header = True).load
('/home/ds/data/DW/ratings.csv')
data.show()
```

输出结果如下:

```
+------+-------+------+---------+
|userId|movieId|rating|timestamp|
+------+-------+------+---------+
|     1|      1|   4.0|964982703|
|     1|      3|   4.0|964981247|
|     1|      6|   4.0|964982224|
|     1|     47|   5.0|964983815|
|     1|     50|   5.0|964982931|
|     1|     70|   3.0|964982400|
|     1|    101|   5.0|964980868|
|     1|    110|   4.0|964982176|
|     1|    151|   5.0|964984041|
|     1|    157|   5.0|964984100|
|     1|    163|   5.0|964983650|
|     1|    216|   5.0|964981208|
|     1|    223|   3.0|964980985|
|     1|    231|   5.0|964981179|
|     1|    235|   4.0|964980908|
|     1|    260|   5.0|964981680|
|     1|    296|   3.0|964982967|
|     1|    316|   3.0|964982310|
|     1|    333|   5.0|964981179|
|     1|    349|   4.0|964982563|
+------+-------+------+---------+
only showing top 20 rows
# 改变数据类型
data = data.withColumn('userId',data['userId'].cast(IntegerType()))
data = data.withColumn('movieId',data['movieId'].cast(IntegerType()))
data = data.withColumn('rating',data['rating'].cast(DoubleType()))
```

```python
# 切分训练集和测试集
(trainingData,testData) = data.randomSplit([0.8,0.2])

# 构建评估模型
als = ALS(maxIter= 10,regParam= 0.1,userCol= 'userId',itemCol= 'movieId',ratingCol= 'rating',coldStartStrategy= 'drop')

# 拟合数据
model = als.fit(trainingData)

# 得到预测值
predictions = model.transform(testData)

# 构建一个评估器,评估标准设置为 rmse,即均方误差
evaluator = RegressionEvaluator(predictionCol= 'prediction',labelCol= 'rating',metricName= 'rmse')

rmse = evaluator.evaluate(predictions)
print(rmse)

# 找出向每个人推荐的前 10 部电影
user_recommendation = model.recommendForAllUsers(10)
user_recommendation.take(2)

# 类似的,找出每部电影最适合推荐的 10 个人
movie_recommendation = model.recommendForAllItems(10)
movie_recommendation.take(2)

# 停止实验
spark.stop()
```

四、练习题

(1)协同过滤的核心理念是什么?

参见算法介绍部分。即根据自己的兴趣爱好,找出与自己兴趣相近的人,然后将他们的选择内容推荐给我。

(2)在 pyspark 中如何实现数据类型转换?例如:如何将 userId 一列改为整数型?

data = data.withColumn('userId',data['userId'].cast(IntegerType()))

第七章 大数据可视化

实验 15 大数据可视化
——使用 matplotlib 进行可视化操作练习

一、实验介绍

matplotlib 库可提供强大的绘图功能,它的配置存储在文件 matplotlibrc 中,使用 matplotlib 时会从配置文件读取默认属性。

有时需要临时使用自定义属性,本实验将练习通过应用程序代码修改 matplotlib 的相关属性值。

属性值参照:matplotlib_customizing。

二、实验要求

(1)掌握 matplotlib 库文件的导入方法。
(2)掌握 matplotlib 的使用代码修改参数配置的两种方法。
(3)掌握 matplotlib 重置配置参数的方法。
(4)掌握 matplotlib 配置画布和字体大小的方法。
(5)掌握 matplotlib 配置线条(粗细、颜色)的方法。
(6)掌握 matplotlib 配置点图(形状)的方法。
(7)了解 matplotlib 的默认参数读取方法。
(8)了解 matplotlib 的配置文件。

三、实验步骤

完成下面设置的练习任务,操作提示用于作业参考。

练习任务 1:导入 matplotlib 库文件

要使用 matplotlib,需先导入 matplotlib 库文件,建议同时导入 matplotlib.pyplot、numpy 和 scipy 库备用。

为了方便在 jupyter notebook 中显示图形文件,还需要用魔法命令将图形嵌入到 notebook 中。

操作提示:

```python
import numpy as np
import scipy as sp
import matplotlib as mpl
import matplotlib.pyplot as plt

% matplotlib inline

# 绘制图形测试
plt.plot(range(5))


### 输入你的作业代码 ###



### 作业代码结束 ###
```

练习任务 2：matplotlib 的使用代码修改参数配置的两种方法

要求：修改图像字体大小为 20

操作提示：

方法一：使用参数字典'rcParams'访问并修改所有已经加载的配置项。

方法二：通过向 matplotlib.rc() 传入属性的关键字元组来修改配置项。

```python
# 方法一：
mpl.rcParams['font.size'] = 20
plt.plot(range(5))


# 方法二：
mpl.rc('font', size = 12)
plt.plot(range(5))



### 输入你的作业代码 ###




### 作业代码结束 ###
```

练习任务 3:重置 matplotlib 参数配置

重置动态修改后的 maplotlib 配置参数。

操作提示:

```
mpl.rcdefaults()
plt.plot(range(5))
```

```
###输入你的作业代码###




### 作业代码结束###
```

练习任务 4:matplotlib 配置画布和字体大小

画布大小的属性是 figure.figsize,需要输入一个元组(宽度、高度)设置宽度和高度,默认单位是英寸。

字体大小使的属性是 font.size,默认大小是 10pt。控制图形中所有的字体,包含(tick labels, axes, labels, title, etc)。

要求:

(1)将画布修改为 5×7 inches。

(2)将字号修改为 6。

操作提示(从本任务起:下面将提示 rcParams 的参数字典方法,建议自己摸索 rc 的方法)。

```
mpl.rcParams['figure.figsize'] = (5,3)
mpl.rcParams['font.size'] = 6
plt.plot(range(5))
```

```
###输入你的作业代码###




### 作业代码结束###
```

练习任务 5：配置 matplotlib 线条（粗细、颜色）

线条的粗细的属性是 lines.linewidth，默认粗细 1.5。

线条颜色的属性配置已经由 lines.color 统一到 axes.prop_cycle，是一个颜色的循环配置。

操作提示：

将线条粗细修改为 10。

线条颜色修改为蓝色 b。

```
mpl.rcParams['lines.linewidth'] = 10

# 老版 matplotlib 使用:mpl.rcParams['lines.color'] = 'b'配置为 blue 蓝色
mpl.rcParams['axes.prop_cycle'] = mpl.cycler(color= ["b", "# e94cdc", "0.7"])

plt.plot(range(5))
```

```
# # # 输入你的作业代码 # # #




# # # 作业代码结束 # # #
```

练习任务 6：配置 matplotlib 散点图（点的形状）

散点图中点的形状的属性是 scatter.marker，默认的 marker 是 'o'

marker 的形状介绍如下：

marker 的形状要求：

(1)将 marker 修改为"点"。

(2)将 marker 修改为"正三角形"。

第七章 大数据可视化

附录六　Marker 属性：

marker	description	描述
"."	point	点
","	pixel	像素
"o"	circle	圈
"v"	triangle_down	倒三角形
"^"	triangle_up	正三角形
"<"	triangle_left	左三角形
">"	triangle_right	右三角形
"1"	tri_down	tri_down
"2"	tri_up	tri_up
"3"	tri_left	tri_left
"4"	tri_right	tri_right
"8"	octagon	八角形
"s"	square	正方形
"p"	pentagon	五角
"*"	star	星星
"h"	hexagon1	六角1
"H"	hexagon2	六角2
"+"	plus	加号
"x"	x	x号
"D"	diamond	钻石
"d"	thin_diamond	细钻
"|"	vline	v线
"_"	hline	H线
TICKLEFT	tickleft	左刻度
TICKRIGHT	tickright	右刻度
TICKUP	tickup	上刻度
TICKDOWN	tickdown	下刻度
CARETLEFT	caretleft	caretleft
CARETRIGHT	caretright	caretright
CARETUP	caretup	caretup
CARETDOWN	caretdown	caretdown

"None"	nothing	无
None	nothing	无
" "	nothing	无
""	nothing	无
'$...$'	render the string using mathtext.	使用 mathtext 渲染的字符串。
verts	a list of (x, y) pairs used for Path vertices.	用于路径顶点（X，Y）对的列表。
path	a Path instance.	一个路径实例。
(numsides, style, angle)	see below	

操作提示：

绘制散点图的语句：plt.scatter(x=range(5),y=[np.random.random() * num for num in range(5)])。

提示代码：

```
mpl.rcParams['scatter.marker'] = '*'
plt.scatter(x= range(5),y= [np.random.random()* num for num in range(5)])
```

```
### 输入你的作业代码 ###



### 作业代码结束 ###
```

实验 16　大数据可视化实战案例
——利用 matplotlib 分析自行车租赁情况

一、实验介绍

UCI 自行车租赁数据集基于 Capital Bikeshare 公司的实际数据,该公司维护着美国华盛顿特区的自行车租赁网络。

二、实验要求

(1)实现风格参数的配置。
(2)实现关联分析。
(3)实现分布分析。
(4)实现组间分析。

三、实验步骤

完成下面设置的练习任务,操作提示用于作业参考。

开始试验练习步骤前,请先执行下方代码,以确保 pandas、numpy 和 seaborn 的正常调用。

```
# loading
% matplotlib inline
import numpy as np
import pandas as pd
import matplotlib.pyplot as plt
import seaborn as sns


daily_path = '/home/ds/data/Bike-Sharing-Dataset/day.csv'
daily_data = pd.read_csv(daily_path) # 读取 csv 文件
daily_data['dteday'] = pd.to_datetime(daily_data['dteday']) # 把字符串数据传换成日期数据
drop_list = ['instant', 'season', 'yr', 'mnth', 'holiday', 'workingday', 'weathersit', 'atemp', 'hum'] # 不关注的列
daily_data.drop(drop_list, inplace = True, axis = 1) # inplace= true 在对象上直接操作


daily_data.head() # 看一看数据哈~
```

练习任务 1:风格参数配置

(1)设置 seaborn 的风格为白底无格风格。
(2)设置调色板为 husl 颜色系统的 10 色。
根据预定义 daily_data 数据集完成本练习。
操作提示:

```
sns.set_style("white")
sns.set_palette(sns.color_palette("husl", 10)) # http://www.hsluv.org
```

```
# # # 输入你的作业代码 # # #



# # # 作业代码结束 # # #
```

练习任务 2:关联分析

利用 sns.lmplot() 和其句柄下 set_size_inches() 函数,绘制温度(temp)和租车量(cnt)的关联分析图,并设置画布大小为 14×7 inches。
根据预定义 daily_data 数据集完成本练习。
操作提示:

```
g = sns.lmplot(x= "temp", y= "cnt", data= daily_data)
g.fig.set_size_inches(14, 7)
g.set_axis_labels('Normalized temperature (C)', 'Check outs')
```

```
# # # 输入你的作业代码 # # #



# # # 作业代码结束 # # #
```

练习任务 3:分布分析

(1)利用 sns.distplot() 函数分别对总租车量(cnt)、散客租车量(casual)和注册客户租车量(registered)的分布进行分析,并绘制在一张图中。
(2)利用 sns.jointplot() 函数对散客租车量(casual)和注册客户租车量(registered)两个特征绘制 kde 核密度关系图。
根据预定义 daily_data 数据集完成本练习。

操作提示:

```
# 1
sns.distplot(daily_data["casual"])        # 红色    类似指数衰减
sns.distplot(daily_data["cnt"])           # 绿色
sns.distplot(daily_data["registered"])    # 蓝色    类似正态分布
# 要是发现有的图形显示不全,就先画那个显示不全的图形在画布上
plt.show()
# 2
sns.jointplot(data= daily_data, x= "registered", y= "casual", kind= "kde")
plt.show()
```

```
# # # 输入你的作业代码 # # #



# # # 作业代码结束 # # #
```

练习任务 4:组间分析

利用 sns.boxplot() 函数绘制注册客户租车量(registered)在一周各天(weekday)里的分布箱型图。

根据预定义 daily_data 数据集完成本练习。

操作提示:

```
sns.boxplot(data= daily_data, x= "weekday", y= "registered")
```

```
# # # 输入你的作业代码 # # #



# # # 作业代码结束 # # #
```

四、练习题

(1)绘制总租车量(cnt)和一周内各天(weekday)的分布箱式图。

输入你的作业代码

作业代码结束

(2)查找箱式图中各个部分的含义。

上界限：

下界限：

箱子宽度：

箱子上限：

箱子下限：

离群点：

(3)绘制出每一天中租车总量(cnt)与温度(temp)的线性图。

要求：绘制在一张图表中。

操作提示：使用 hue 参数/

输入你的作业代码

作业代码结束